BOOST YOUR CONFIDENCE

BOOST YOUR CONFIDENCE

42 DAYS TO A NEW YOU

JASMINE WILLIAMS

TABLE OF CONTENTS

UNDERSTANDING CONFIDENCE: MORE THAN JUST A FEELING

Confidence is not merely a transient emotional state; it is a potent inner force that influences our actions, decisions, and interactions. In this chapter, we will delve into the science of confidence, practical ways to cultivate it, and the importance of assessing and maintaining confidence over time.

The Science Behind It

Confidence is rooted in the psychological and physiological processes of the human body. Scientific studies have shown that confidence can be intertwined with a variety of factors, including:

- **Neurochemical Levels:** Certain hormones like serotonin and oxytocin are related to feelings of self-esteem and social confidence, while cortisol and adrenaline may be linked to stress and anxiety.

- **Brain Structure:** The amygdala and the prefrontal cortex play significant roles in managing fear and confidence. A well-balanced interaction between these areas can lead to a healthier confidence level.

- **Body Language:** Your posture and gestures can not only reflect but also influence your confidence levels due to the concept of 'embodied cognition.'

Incorporating the science of confidence into your daily life can lead to meaningful changes in how you perceive yourself and interact with the world.

Practical Implementation

To build confidence effectively, consider adopting the following strategies:

1. **Positive Self-Talk:** Replace negative thoughts with positive affirmations. Be your own encouraging coach.

2. **Goal Setting:** Establish clear, attainable goals. Achieving them can provide a sense of accomplishment and boost your self-confidence.

3. **Skill Development:** Invest time in learning and mastering new skills. Competence breeds confidence.

4. **Healthy Lifestyle Choices:** Exercise, nutrition, and adequate sleep can improve your overall well-being and, in turn, your confidence levels.

Illustration: Jane, a budding entrepreneur, once doubted her decision-making skills. By acknowledging her past successes and setting small, achievable targets, she gradually bolstered her confidence and now runs a successful local business.

Consistency and Evaluation

Maintaining confidence is a continuous process. It is crucial to:

• **Monitor Your Progress:** Keep a journal to track your confidence levels and the situations that affect them.

• **Seek Feedback:** Constructive criticism from trusted peers can provide insights and help you improve steadily.

- **Adjust Your Strategies:** Be flexible and willing to adapt your methods as you learn more about what works for you.

Regular reflection and evaluation are key in ensuring that your confidence remains strong and resilient through life's ebbs and flows.

By understanding the complexities of confidence and taking deliberate steps to foster it, we can all unlock a more assured and assertive version of ourselves. Remember, confidence is a journey, not just a destination.

THE SCIENCE OF SELF-ESTEEM: WHY IT MATTERS

Self-esteem not only shapes our navigation through the social world but also affects how high we set the bar for our achievements and the joy we derive from our everyday lives. Let's delve into the mechanics of self-worth and how you can harness its power on your journey to confidence and personal growth.

The Science Behind It

Understanding the Foundations of Self-Esteem

Self-esteem is an internal evaluation of one's own worth. It is shaped by a variety of factors, including the approval of others, success and failure, and personal beliefs.

- **Biological Factors**: Our brains come hard-wired to seek social validation as a means of survival. Neurotransmitters and hormones play roles in how we perceive our social status and self-worth.

- **Psychological Factors**: It encompasses cognitive aspects, such as beliefs and perceptions about oneself, which have been shaped through personal experiences and developmental history.

The Impact on Well-being

Research shows that healthy self-esteem correlates with mental sturdiness, resilience, and an overall positive outlook on life, whereas low self-esteem can lead to psychological issues like depression and anxiety.

Practical Implementation

Building a Foundation

Practical implementation is about transforming the knowledge of self-esteem into everyday habits.

- **Positive Affirmations**: Remind yourself of your strengths and successes. Constructive self-talk can build a mental foundation of positive self-regard.

- **Goal-Setting**: Set realistic, achievable goals. Celebrate the small victories on the way to larger achievements.

- **Self-Reflection**: Evaluate your core beliefs and challenge the negative ones. Reflect on experiences with a learning mindset rather than a self-critical one.

Developing Healthy Relationships

Components of high self-esteem often stem from our relationships and how we interact with others.

- **Supportive Social Circles**: Surround yourself with people who lift you up and foster an environment of mutual respect.

- **Boundary Setting**: Learn to say no and articulate your needs in relationships to prevent resentment and loss of self-esteem.

Consistency and Evaluation

Maintaining and nurturing self-esteem requires consistency and regular evaluation of strategies.

- **Consistency**:

  - **Routine**: Establish a daily routine that includes self-esteem boosting activities.

  - **Adaptability**: Be willing to adapt your strategies as you grow and face new circumstances.

- **Evaluation**:

  - **Regular Check-ins**: Set aside time to reflect on your self-worth and progress.

  - **Seek Feedback**: Sometimes, feedback from trusted friends or mentors can offer invaluable insight into how we are perceived and may help us adjust our self-esteem strategies.

Remember, the journey to improved self-esteem is a marathon, not a sprint. It requires patience, persistence, and a pinch of courage. Equip yourself with the knowledge of why self-esteem matters, implement these strategies consistently, and periodically evaluate your growth. In doing so, you'll build a robust sense of self that illuminates every aspect of your life, paving the way for unimagined successes and contentment.

THE MYTH OF INBORN CONFIDENCE: DEBUNKING PERVASIVE MYTHS

Confidence is often seen as an innate characteristic, something that people are either born with or without. This chapter aims to dismantle that myth and provide practical steps to nurture and build confidence over time. Understand that confidence, like any other skill, can be developed with intention and effort.

The Science Behind It

Recent psychological studies have shown that confidence is not purely inborn but is heavily influenced by our experiences, environment, and personal growth. Factors such as our upbringing, the praise we receive, and how we're treated by peers all contribute to the development of our self-esteem.

- Neuroplasticity, the brain's ability to change and adapt throughout life, supports the idea that we can develop confidence. Each time we step out of our comfort zone and have a positive experience, our brain records a victory.

- The concept of "self-efficacy" introduced by psychologist Albert Bandura indicates that observing others succeed and succeeding in our own endeavors can bolster our belief in our abilities.

• Repeated exposure to challenges helps build a "confidence muscle," just as exercise strengthens our physical muscles.

Practical Implementation

Building real, lasting confidence requires a deliberate approach. Here are practical steps to consider:

1. **Set Achievable Goals**: Success breeds confidence. Start with small, attainable goals and gradually increase the difficulty. Each success will lay a brick on the pathway to greater self-assurance.

2. **Embrace a Growth Mindset**: Believe in your ability to improve and learn. Instead of shying away from challenges, view them as opportunities to grow.

3. **Positive Affirmations**: Implement daily affirmations. Positive self-talk can rewire your brain to be more confident.

4. **Surround Yourself with Positivity**: The company you keep can influence your self-perception. Find peers and mentors who uplift you.

5. **Learn from Failure**: See failure as part of the learning process. Reflect on what went wrong, adapt, and try again with a better strategy.

Example: Imagine a young employee aspiring to lead a project. Initially, self-doubt creeps in, but through setting small goals, seeking feedback, and achieving smaller milestones, the employee's confidence grows, readying them for bigger challenges.

Consistency and Evaluation

Building confidence is an ongoing process. It requires consistent practice and reflection.

- **Track Progress**: Keep a journal detailing your confidence-building activities and their outcomes. This helps in recognizing patterns and reinforcing positive behaviors.

- **Seek Feedback**: Constructive criticism can be invaluable for growth. Just ensure it's from trusted sources who have your best interests at heart.

- **Resilience**: Understand that not every day will be a win. Learn to bounce back with resilience, viewing setbacks as temporary.

Illustration: Consider the story of a writer who was once terrified of sharing her work. By consistently submitting stories despite rejections and learning from the critiques, the writer's confidence in her craft improved over time.

Conclusion

Shed the belief in the myth of inborn confidence. Recognize that confidence can be developed through thoughtful, deliberate actions and a commitment to personal growth. Remember, the journey to becoming confident is a marathon, not a sprint, and every step forward is a triumph.

THE ART OF SELF-COMPASSION: BEING KIND TO YOURSELF

The Science Behind It

Self-compassion is a construct that has garnered considerable attention in psychology over the past two decades, largely due to the work of Dr. Kristin Neff and other scholars in the field. Central to self-compassion is treating oneself with kindness, understanding, and support in the face of mistakes, failures, and perceived inadequacies—just as you would treat a good friend.

The Three Key Components

1. **Self-Kindness**: This is about being gentle and understanding with oneself rather than harshly critical or judgmental.

2. **Common Humanity**: It involves recognizing that suffering and personal inadequacy are part of the shared human experience – something we all go through rather than being something that happens to "me" alone.

3. **Mindfulness**: This means being aware of the present moment and one's painful feelings without over-identifying with them.

Neuroscientific studies suggest that self-compassion can positively affect the brain's circuitry related to emotions like empathy and can decrease the intensity of the brain's threat response, which can make us less defensive and more open to learning from our experiences.

The Benefits

Evidence shows that individuals who practice self-compassion tend to enjoy:

- Lower levels of anxiety and depression

- Enhanced emotional resilience

- Better physical health

- More satisfying personal relationships

Practical Implementation

Transforming insight into action is essential. Here are practical steps you can take to cultivate self-compassion:

Starting Small

- **Mindful Breathing**: Begin by taking a few minutes each day to focus on your breath, acknowledging your feelings without judgment.

- **Self-Compassion Break**: Whenever you find yourself in a moment of distress, pause and offer yourself words of comfort, as you would to a friend.

Communicating with Yourself

- **Positive Self-Talk**: Change the dialogue in your head. Swap self-criticism for compassionate self-talk.

- **Write a Compassion Letter**: Pen a letter to yourself from the perspective of a loving friend.

Daily Practices

- **Gratitude Journaling**: At the end of each day, write down things you're grateful for about yourself.

- **Guided Meditations**: Utilize guided self-compassion meditations and exercises available in books or online.

Consistency and Evaluation

Like any skill, self-compassion requires consistent practice.

Creating a Routine

- **Set Aside Time**: Dedicate a daily time for self-compassion exercises.

- **Reminder Triggers**: Use regular cues (like meal times) to remind you to practice self-kindness.

Assessing Your Progress

- **Reflect Daily**: Take a few minutes each evening to reflect on your self-compassion practices.

- **Seek Feedback**: Share your journey with a friend or join a community that supports personal growth.

Finally, re-evaluate your self-compassion levels after 42 days. Have you noticed a shift in how you react to failures? Are you kinder to yourself? Adjust your practices as necessary, keeping in mind that the ultimate goal is to integrate self-compassion into your very being.

IDENTIFYING PERSONAL STRENGTHS: THE BUILDING BLOCKS OF CONFIDENCE

The Science Behind It

Confidence doesn't materialize out of thin air. It's constructed, akin to a skillful architect drafting a sturdy and impressive building. The foundation? Our personal strengths. So, let's don our lab coats and dissect the science behind this.

Psychological Research

Studies in positive psychology demonstrate that individuals who recognize and harness their unique strengths:

- Tend to be more satisfied with their lives

- Often report higher levels of well-being

- Are typically more resilient in the face of stress

The VIA Classification

At the core of this is the VIA Institute's classification, a renowned catalog of character strengths that has empirical backing. It elucidates 24 personal strengths, neatly categorized under six broad virtues.

Neurological Perspectives

Brain imaging studies highlight how positive self-affirmation — that is, the recognition of one's own strengths — can affect the neural pathways associated with positivity and self-value.

Practical Implementation

So how does one unearth these gems of strengths lodged within? Let's rummage together with some hands-on tactics.

Identifying Your Strengths

1. **Reflect on Past Successes**:

   ○ Think about instances when you felt proud and determine the strengths you used.

2. **Ask for Feedback**:

   ○ Sometimes, friends and colleagues are like mirrors reflecting strengths we didn't know shone so bright.

3. **Take a Strengths Assessment**:

   ○ Tools like the VIA Survey provide a structured way to uncover your strengths.

Developing Confidence Through Strengths

- **Utilize Your Strengths**:

   ○ Find activities that let your strengths shimmer. Success in these will plant the seeds of confidence.

- **Create 'Strengths Statements'**:

  - Frame positive affirmations around your strengths. Repeat them; let your mind marinate in them.

Examples for Clarity

- Mia discovered her knack for empathy. She thrives in roles that require active listening and emotional support.

- Jack unearthed his strength in strategic planning. He began volunteering for project management tasks, boosting his confidence.

Consistency and Evaluation

Identifying your strengths is akin to planting a seed—it needs nurturing to grow into the robust tree of confidence.

Strategies for Consistency

1. **Daily Strength Application**:

   - Purposefully integrate your strengths into your daily routine.

2. **Strength-Based Goals**:

   - Set goals that nurture and display your strengths. Climbing these step by step builds a sturdy ladder of confidence.

3. **Strengths Journal**:

   - Keep a log of how you use your strengths—one small entry a day can illuminate your growth over time.

Periodic Evaluation

- Revisit and re-assess your strengths periodically. Growth changes us, and our strengths mature with us.

Real-Life Success:

- Amit kept a journal, noting his use of creativity in problem-solving at work. Reading his progress over six months filled him with pride (and confidence).

By closely adhering to this framework, every reader can become their own strength-detector and architect of confidence. Remember, knowing your strengths isn't boastful—it's the bedrock of a confident life.

THE CONFIDENCE-SELF-ESTEEM CONNECTION: HOW THEY INTERACT

The Science Behind It

Confidence and self-esteem are often used interchangeably, but they are, in fact, distinct constructs that interact in meaningful ways. Imagine self-esteem as the foundation of a house—how we feel about ourselves at the core—and confidence as the structure built upon it, which is how we project ourselves in specific situations.

- **Self-Esteem** is the internal sense of worth or value we assign to ourselves. It's stable and encompasses our beliefs about our value and adequacy as individuals.

- **Confidence**, on the other hand, is situation-specific, dynamic, and reflects our beliefs in our abilities to succeed at a task.

While self-esteem is like the bedrock of our psychological makeup, confidence is the weather vane, spinning with the winds of our experiences. Research in psychology suggests that those with high self-esteem find it easier to develop confidence. On the other hand, consistently displaying confidence, particularly in conquering challenging tasks, can bolster our self-esteem—creating a beneficial cycle.

A key hormone in this interplay is serotonin, sometimes known as the 'confidence chemical'. It regulates mood and is tied to feelings of self-worth and competence. Low serotonin levels are associated with depression, which often features low self-esteem.

Practical Implementation

To bolster the connection between confidence and self-esteem, we can adopt certain practices:

- **Positive Self-Talk**: Cultivating a positive internal dialogue can strengthen self-esteem, which in turn, fuels confidence.

    - Begin each day by affirming your worth with statements like, "I am capable and deserving of success."

    - Replace negative thoughts with positive ones. Instead of "I can't do this," say "I will learn how to do this."

- **Skill Development**: Confidence is often tied to competence in specific areas.

    - Identify skills related to your goals and take steps to refine or learn them.

    - Celebrate small wins in skill acquisition to build confidence.

- **Social Feedback**: Constructive feedback can significantly influence our self-esteem and confidence.

    - Seek out mentors, friends, or colleagues who can provide honest, positive feedback on your abilities and progress.

    - Learn to accept compliments graciously; they are affirmations of your capabilities.

Consistency and Evaluation

The cultivation of confidence and self-esteem is not a one-time event but a consistent effort.

1. **Set Small, Achievable Goals**: This provides a roadmap for success, building confidence with each step.

2. **Reflect on Your Progress**: Regularly assess how far you've come and the areas where you've seen improvement.

3. **Journaling**: Keeping a journal to track successes and feelings can help in recognizing patterns and reinforcing progress.

Consider the story of Sarah, a fledgling writer who struggled with low self-esteem. By setting a goal to write daily, seeking constructive feedback, and journaling her experiences, Sarah gradually saw her confidence in her writing abilities soar. This, in turn, reinforced her self-esteem, creating a positive feedback loop. Remember, the connection between confidence and self-esteem is synergistic. They feed into each other, so focus on building both simultaneously to maximize personal growth. Aim for progress, not perfection, and embrace the journey of self-improvement with an understanding that each step forward is a victory in its own right.

SETTING THE STAGE: DEFINING YOUR GOALS FOR GROWTH

In the realm of personal development, crafting a vision for your growth is akin to plotting a course on a map; without a destination in mind, it's easy to wander aimlessly. This chapter focuses on the foundational step of setting clear, achievable goals that will steer your journey towards heightened confidence, enriched self-esteem, and holistic personal growth. Let's dive in and explore how you can translate your aspirations into reality.

The Science Behind It

*Neuroplasticity * is a fundamental concept that underscores our ability to change and adapt. Neuroscience has shown that our brains are capable of forming new connections and patterns of thought throughout our lives. When we set specific goals:

- We give direction to this potential for change.

- Our focus narrows, allowing for more effective use of our mental resources.

- With repetition, these focused thoughts and actions forge new neural pathways, bolstering our capacity to achieve our goals.

Goal-Setting Theory, developed by psychologists Edwin Locke and Gary Latham, posits that high-performance goals can lead to higher performance as compared to easy or vague goals. This theory highlights the importance of setting goals that are:

- **Specific**: Clearly defining what you wish to achieve.

- **Measurable**: Having criteria to track your progress.

- **Achievable**: Setting goals that are realistic and attainable.

- **Relevant**: Ensuring that the goals are pertinent to your values and long-term objectives.

- **Time-bound**: Having a deadline to add a sense of urgency and focus.

In aligning your objectives with these criteria, you establish a framework that enables not just growth but also a means to measure and appreciate your progress.

Practical Implementation

1. **Identify Your Core Values**:

   - Reflect on what matters most to you.

   - Consider the areas where you seek improvement in confidence and self-esteem.

2. **Articulate Your Vision**:

   - Envision your best self – who are you when you carry yourself with confidence?

   - Write a personal mission statement that encapsulates your aspirations.

3. **Establish Specific Goals**:

   - Break down your vision into tangible goals.

   - Use the SMART criteria as a guide.

4. **Plan Your Actions**:

   ○ Determine the steps needed to achieve each goal.

   ○ Set milestones and checkpoints to maintain momentum.

5. **Equip Yourself with Resources**:

   ○ Seek knowledge and tools that facilitate personal growth.

   ○ Consider books, courses, mentors, or support groups.

6. **Visualize Success**:

   ○ Regularly imagine achieving your goals.

   ○ Use visualization as a tool to reinforce your commitment.

Consistency and Evaluation

Maintaining a constant pace towards your goals and regularly assessing your progress are critical elements in your transformation journey. Here's how:

• **Set Daily Intentions**: Begin each day with clarity by setting intentions that align with your goals.

• **Track Progress**: Keep a journal or use an app to monitor your advancements and setbacks.

• **Adjust as Necessary**: Be prepared to modify your goals if circumstances change or new insights emerge.

• **Celebrate Milestones**: Recognize and celebrate your achievements to boost morale and commitment.

Remember that growth is not always linear. Embrace the ebbs and flows as learning experiences and trust in your ability to proceed. By incorporating the science-backed strategies of goal setting, embracing practical steps, ensuring consistency, and performing regular evaluations, you'll be well on your way to enhancing your confidence and embarking on a powerful journey of personal transformation. Keep turning the pages, and let's continue to discover how to unlock the new you, one confident step at a time.

QUIETING THE INNER CRITIC: STRATEGIES FOR POSITIVE SELF-TALK

Our inner critic can be a dominant force, often hindering our confidence and self-esteem. Understanding how it works and learning to manage it through positive self-talk is an essential step towards personal growth. In this chapter, we will delve into the science that unpacks the mechanisms of our inner dialogue, explore practical steps to shift our self-talk from negative to positive, and discuss how to gauge progress through consistent practice and evaluation.

The Science Behind It

The mind is an incredibly powerful tool, often conjuring a stream of consciousness that can be both beneficial and detrimental. The inner critic is part of this mental chatter, born out of our experiences, fears, and societal pressures. Let's unpack the science:

- **Neural Pathways**: Repetitive negative self-talk can strengthen certain neural pathways, effectively ingraining these patterns within our brain circuitry.

- **Stress and the Brain**: Persistent negativity can lead to increased levels of stress hormones like cortisol, which can hamper cognitive function and emotional well-being.

- **Self-Perception**: Our internal dialogue directly impacts how we perceive ourselves, which in turn can affect our behavior and decision-making processes.

Practical Implementation

Turning the tables on the inner critic requires intentional action. Here are actionable steps to initiate positive self-talk:

1. **Awareness is Key**: Begin by simply noticing when your inner critic shows up. What events trigger it? What form does it take?

2. **Challenge Negative Thoughts**: When you catch yourself in a spiral of negative self-talk, pause and challenge these thoughts. Are they really true?

3. **Affirmations and Mantras**: Create personal affirmations that counteract the critic. Repeat them daily.

4. **Visualization**: Visualizing success and positive outcomes can reinforce a positive mindset.

5. **Surround Yourself with Positivity**: Engage with positive people and consume uplifting content.

6. **Gratitude Practice**: Regularly reflecting on things you're grateful for can shift focus from negative to positive thinking.

Consistency and Evaluation

Like any skill, positive self-talk requires consistent practice. Here's how to stay on track and evaluate your progress:

- **Set aside time for self-reflection**: Daily or weekly, take a moment to reflect on your self-talk patterns.

- **Journaling**: Keep a journal to track changes in your thoughts and feelings.

• **Seek Feedback**: Sometimes, external perspectives from trusted friends or mentors can help you see progress.

• **Adjust as Needed**: As you evaluate, be willing to adjust your strategies to find what works best for you.

• **Celebrate Small Wins**: Recognizing even the smallest improvements can be a great motivator.

Let's sprinkle in a real-life example to illustrate these points. Imagine Sarah, a young entrepreneur, who realized her inner critic was saying, "You're not experienced enough to succeed." Applying the practical steps, she became aware of this pattern, challenged its validity, and replaced it with a new affirmation, "I am fully capable and can learn anything I need to succeed." Over time, Sarah saw a noticeable change in her confidence and decision-making. Throughout these pages, you'll find narratives like Sarah's and other practical illustrations to show how these strategies come to life. You'll gather not only the knowledge but also the encouragement to embark on a journey of silencing the inner critic and fostering an empowering internal dialogue that supports your growth.

Remember, it's not about muting the inner critic indefinitely— sometimes, its job is to keep us in check. But it's about transforming it into a voice that also sees and reinforces our potential, leading us to a more confident and positive self. Aim to make positive self-talk not just a practice, but a way of being, laying down the foundation for a truly new you.

HARNESSING THE POWER OF VISUALIZATION: SEEING YOUR CONFIDENT SELF

The Science Behind It

Visualization is not just a motivational tool; it's a cognitive function that can lead to real, tangible changes in our lives. To understand the power of visualization, let's delve into its scientific basis:

- **Neuroplasticity**: Our brains have the remarkable ability to form new neural connections throughout life. Visualization has been shown to strengthen these connections, effectively rewiring our brain towards the traits and behaviors we imagine.

- **Mirror Neurons**: These are neurons that fire both when a person acts and when they observe the same action performed by another. When we visualize ourselves acting confidently, these neurons may fire in patterns similar to those utilized during the actual confident behavior, this primes the brain for action.

- **Emotional Regulation**: Visualization can impact our emotional state. By imagining ourselves in a state of confidence, we can begin to invoke the feelings associated with it, which could translate to an actual boost in confidence real-life situations.

• **The Reticular Activating System (RAS)**: This is the part of your brain that filters and directs your attention. When you focus on your confident self through visualization, you train your RAS to recognize and prioritize confidence-boosting opportunities and behaviors in your daily life.

Practical Implementation

How do we put this into practice? Here's a straightforward approach:

1. **Find a Quiet Space**: Distraction-free environments help in creating vivid visualizations.

2. **Define Your Confident Self**: Clearly envision what confidence looks like for you—how you stand, speak, and interact with others.

3. **Engage All Your Senses**: A powerful visualization involves all senses — what do you see, hear, and feel?

4. **Create a Routine**: Regular visualization sessions increase their effectiveness.

5. **Incorporate Affirmations**: Positive affirmations can reinforce the confident behaviors you're visualizing.

Let's consider an example. Imagine you're going to give a presentation. Visualize the scene in detail: the room layout, the audience's faces, the smooth tone of your voice as you speak, the feeling of the pointer in your hand, and the confidence with which you answer questions.

Consistency and Evaluation

Finally, consistency is key, and evaluation allows you to fine-tune your visualization practice. Make it a daily habit and assess its impact:

- **Track Your Progress**: Keep a log or journal of your visualization experiences and any outcomes you notice in relation to your confidence levels.

- **Adjust as Necessary**: If certain visualizations don't seem to be having the desired effect, adjust the details or script until it feels more genuine and effective.

- **Test in Small Steps**: Start by applying your newfound confidence in low-risk situations and gradually take on more challenging ones.

Remember, visualization is a skill that improves with time and practice. It's not about immediate perfection, but rather gradual and continuous improvement.

To summarize, harnessing the power of visualization involves understanding its scientific basis, consistently applying practical techniques, and regularly evaluating and adjusting your approach. Through this systematic process, you can shape your confident self not just in your mind's eye but in everyday reality.

THE ROLE OF BODY LANGUAGE IN SELF-ASSURANCE

In the tapestry of human communication, body language is a vivid thread woven deeply into the fabric of our social interactions. It's a silent orchestra that plays a crucial role in the way confidence is perceived and projected. As we embark on a journey to explore this intriguing aspect, let's delve into the science, put these insights into practice, and learn to consistently evaluate our nonverbal cues to bolster self-assurance.

The Science Behind It

Body language is rooted in the deep biological signals of our ancestors — gestures, postures, and movements conveyed vital information that was key to survival. Fast-track to modern times, and these primal signals still hold immense power in our daily engagements.

- **Mirror Neurons and Mimicry**: When we observe confident body language, our brain's mirror neurons activate, causing us to unconsciously emulate the confidence we see. This imitation has the power to bolster our own feeling of self-assurance.

- **Postural Feedback**: Research shows that adopting an expansive posture (open arms and standing tall) can increase levels of testosterone (linked to dominance) and decrease cortisol (associated with stress), making us feel more powerful and in control.

- **Facial Feedback Hypothesis**: Our expressions don't just reflect our emotions; they also contribute to the intensity of our feelings. Smiling, even mechanically, can induce feelings of joy and reduce stress.

Understanding these underlying principles enables us to harness body language's influence over our self-assurance.

Practical Implementation

Putting this knowledge into action, there are several methods we can employ to ensure our body language is conveying confidence:

- **Power Posing**: Before a nerve-racking situation, strike a power pose. Stand with your hands on your hips and your feet shoulder-width apart for two minutes to boost your confidence levels.

- **Eye Contact**: Maintain consistent but comfortable eye contact during conversations. It signals attention, respect, and confidence in the interaction.

- **Gesture with Purpose**: Use your hands to reinforce your points. Controlled and deliberate gestures can help articulate your thoughts more clearly and denote assurance in your speech.

Remember, the goal is not to create a façade of confidence but to let these behaviors guide your internal state towards genuine self-assurance.

Consistency and Evaluation

Enduring change in body language and self-assurance isn't achieved overnight; it requires practice and consistency. As with any skill, the more you practice, the more natural it becomes. Here's how you can ensure that your efforts are yielding results:

1. **Self-assessment**: Keep a journal of occasions where you felt confident versus insecure. Note your body language during each and look for patterns.

2. **Ask for Feedback**: Trustworthy friends or colleagues can offer valuable insights into how your nonverbal cues are perceived.

3. **Record and Observe**: Watching videos of yourself can be eye-opening. It allows you to independently evaluate your body language and make adjustments.

4. **Continual Learning**: Stay updated with the latest research in body language and incorporate new techniques that align with your growth.

Body language is an art, ever-evolving and deeply personal. You're sculpting your expressive self, chiseling away doubt to reveal the assured figure within. Through awareness, application, and assessment, body language becomes not just a tool for self-assurance but an embodiment of it—integral to your journey in "Boost Your Confidence: 42 Days to a New You".

THE SOUND OF CONFIDENCE: FINDING YOUR ASSERTIVE VOICE

The Science Behind It

Understanding the science of confidence and communication isn't just for scholars; it's for anyone who wants to make a real change in the way they interact with the world. Our voice is our instrument for conveying thoughts, emotions, and intentions. When we speak assertively, we're not just sharing words; we're signaling self-assurance and conviction.

The Psychology of Vocal Assertiveness

• **Pitch**: High-pitched voices can be perceived as less confident. Lowering your pitch slightly can signal authority.

• **Volume**: Speaking too softly can imply uncertainty, while too loudly might be seen as aggression. Aim for a clear, firm volume.

• **Cadence**: A steady pace shows control, while too fast might convey nervousness.

Biological Influence

Certain hormones, like cortisol and testosterone, can impact how we project our voice. Lower cortisol levels and balanced testosterone can contribute to a more assertive vocal presence.

Practical Implementation

Incorporating science into daily practice is the key to changing how we sound. Here's how to transform knowledge into action:

Exercises for Voice Control

1. **Breathing Techniques**: Practice diaphragmatic breathing to support your voice.

2. **Vocal Warm-ups**: Use scales and tongue twisters to gain flexibility and control.

3. **Pitch Practice**: Record yourself speaking at different pitches to find your optimal assertive tone.

Communication Strategies

• **Stay Present**: Focus on the here and now to maintain a steady voice.

• **Be Concise**: Use clear, direct statements to convey your message without waffling.

• **Pause for Effect**: Silence can be powerful. Use it to emphasize points and to collect your thoughts.

Daily Habits for a Confident Voice

• **Mindful Speech**: Be aware of your speaking habits and actively try to modify them.

• **Positive Affirmations**: Encourage yourself with positive talk to build confidence.

• **Feedback Loop**: Regularly seek constructive feedback on your voice and delivery.

Consistency and Evaluation

Building a consistent habit is essential for long-term change. It takes regular practice and evaluation to adjust and improve.

Regular Practice

• **Schedule Daily Exercises**: Carve out time to practice voice exercises daily.

• **Incorporate into Conversations**: Use every interaction as a chance to practice your assertive voice.

Ongoing Evaluation

• **Self-Assessment**: Regularly record and critique your voice.

• **Ask for Feedback**: Get input from trusted friends, family, or professionals.

When you find the right tone, pace, and volume for your assertive voice, you'll notice a shift, not only in how others perceive you but how you feel about yourself. Embrace this transformative journey with positivity and patience. Remember, the sound of confidence is within your reach.

CULTIVATING A GROWTH MINDSET: EMBRACING CHALLENGES AND CHANGE

Growth is not merely a phase of life; it's a mindset that continuously propels us forward, allowing us to greet the ups and downs with agility and grace. In this journey, you are both the traveler and the mapmaker, charting a course through the unchartered terrains of personal and professional development. But how does one cultivate a mindset that not only withstands but thrives on challenges and change? Let's unpack this.

The Science Behind It

In the landscape of mindset theory, Dr. Carol Dweck's work stands like a lighthouse. Dweck illuminated the contrast between fixed and growth mindsets. While the former perceives abilities as static, the latter sees them as malleable traits that can be developed. Herein lies our interest: the growth mindset.
Brain plasticity, the organ's majestic ability to reorganize itself by forming new neural connections, underpins this mindset. It confirms that our intellectual and emotional faculties are not set in stone but are cultivatable gardens. This growth mindset heralds resilience, a zest for learning, and a hearty embrace of challenges as nutrients for our developmental soil.

- **Neural Growth**: Consistent effort leads to the strengthening of neural pathways.

- **Positive Reinforcement**: Celebrating small wins enhances dopamine release, which encourages persistence.

- **Resilience**: Embracing failures not as defeats but as learning opportunities buffers against adversity.

Practical Implementation

The magic happens in the daily acts. Like a muscle that grows with exercise, a growth mindset strengthens with practice. Below are the tools to seed and water this fertile mindset.

1. **Embrace Imperfections**: Replace the self-criticism for not being perfect with the recognition that imperfections are growth's playgrounds.

2. **Curiosity Over Comfort**: Cultivate curiosity. View challenges as puzzles rather than threats.

3. **Feedback and Reflection**: Seek and reflect on feedback without personalizing it.

4. **Reframe "Failure"**: See setbacks as informative road signs, redirecting your journey rather than ending it.

5. **Set Learning Goals**: Establish goals centered on the acquisition of skills and knowledge rather than just outcomes.

Let's illustrate with an anecdote. Imagine a sales manager facing declining sales, rather than wallowing in distress, the manager seeks feedback, identifies gaps in skills, and enrolls in a marketing strategy course. The challenge becomes a springboard for improvement.

Consistency and Evaluation

Inculcating a growth mindset is not a sprint; it is a marathon. Here's how to keep pace:

• **Track Your Progress**: Keep a journal of your mindset journey. Note the setbacks and how you've approached them.

• **Mindset Milestones**: Establish regular intervals to review and celebrate your mindset milestones.

• **Adjust Your Approach**: Be ready to tweak your strategies if you're not seeing the growth you desire.

Remember, the growth mindset isn't a panacea that transforms challenges into confetti. It's a lens through which adversity appears manageable and even beneficial. It's the steadfast belief that with consistent effort and an openness to learning, your capabilities will stretch, morph, and astonish you and those around you.
As you build your own skyscraper of confidence, let the foundation be a growth mindset, perennially robust and rising proudly towards the expansive sky of your potential. Your exploration of this chapter is a brick in that very foundation. Keep building.

AFFIRMATIONS AND MANTRAS: CONSTRUCTING YOUR CONFIDENCE LEXICON

The Science Behind It

In recent years, psychological research has begun to decode the reasons affirmations and mantras can be powerful tools in our quest for a confident self. At the heart of this practice is the concept of neuroplasticity, the brain's ability to reorganize itself by forming new neural connections throughout life. Here's how affirmations play a role:

- **Repetition and Belief**: When we repeat affirmations, it can strengthen the pathways in our brain associated with the beliefs we're affirming, possibly leading to a more persistent change in our long-term mindset.

- **Self-Affirmation Theory**: This theory suggests that affirming our self-integrity can shield us from the effects of stress and help in facilitating adaptive responses to threats in various spheres of our lives.

- **Positive Self-Visualization**: Mantras and affirmations encourage us to visualize a positive outcome, which can boost our belief in our ability to achieve it. This belief, in turn, can enhance our confidence.

Practical Implementation

Creating your own confidence lexicon involves more than just choosing positive phrases; it's about finding the words that resonate deeply with your personal journey. Let's walk through the process:

1. **Reflection**: Identify the areas of self-doubt or where you seek greater confidence.

2. **Personalization**: Create affirmations that specifically address these areas. Make them personal and in the present tense, as though the quality or success already exists.

3. **Incorporation**: Introduce these mantras into your daily routine. Recite them in front of a mirror, meditate with them, or keep them in view throughout the day.

A morning mantra might sound like, "Today, I trust in my abilities and know that I am capable of greatness." Whereas an evening affirmation could be, "I am grateful for the progress I made today and feel confident in my journey."

Consistency and Evaluation

Establishing a routine is vital when it comes to affirmations. They need to become a part of your daily lexicon. Here's how you can ensure consistency and evaluate their effectiveness:

• **Schedule**: Set aside a specific time each day for your affirmations.

• **Record Keeping**: Maintain a journal to note changes in your mood or confidence levels over time.

• **Adaptability**: Be ready to change affirmations that don't resonate or as your objectives evolve.

By keeping track of your progress, you can adjust affirmations and ensure they remain aligned with your growth and goals.

Remember, constructing a confidence lexicon is akin to planting a garden of self-belief. It requires time, care, and the right conditions to flourish. With dedication to the practice, you can expect to see the blossoms of confidence in every facet of your life.

JOURNALING FOR SELF-DISCOVERY: IDENTIFYING THOUGHT PATTERNS

The Science Behind It

Journaling isn't just a way to record your daily events; it's a gateway to the inner workings of our minds. The practice itself has roots in psychological studies and has been continuously analyzed over the years.

What Research Tells Us:

- **Cognitive Processing**: By writing down our thoughts, we engage multiple cognitive processes, allowing us to examine and organize our thoughts more clearly.

- **Emotional Regulation**: Regular journaling has been linked with improved mood and emotional well-being, by providing an outlet for expressing feelings.

- **Behavioral Insight**: The habit of journaling can reveal patterns in our behavior, which can become the cornerstone for personal development.

Understanding how our thought patterns shape our confidence and self-esteem is integral for personal growth. The process of journaling helps us identify limiting beliefs and the narratives that we tell ourselves, allowing us to rewrite those that hold us back.

Practical Implementation

To incorporate journaling into your regimen for self-discovery, begin by setting aside a few minutes each day to write:

How to Get Started:

1. **Choose Your Medium**: Whether it's a physical notebook or a digital app, select a journaling medium that feels most comfortable and accessible for you.

2. **Create a Habit**: Aim to write regularly, perhaps every morning or evening, to establish a routine.

3. **Be Honest and Unfiltered**: The journal is your private space, so express your thoughts and feelings openly.

What to Write About:

• **Daily Reflections**: What happened during your day and how you felt about it.

• **Gratitude Logs**: Regularly noting what you're thankful for can enhance positivity.

• **Affirmations**: Positive statements that can boost self-esteem.

• **Challenges and Wins**: Documenting your struggles and triumphs can put things in perspective.

Dive Deeper:

• Identify recurring themes or phrases that denote a fixed mindset.

- Recognize triggers that provoke negative self-talk or self-doubt.

- Jot down your accomplishments, however small they may seem.

By implementing these practices, you begin to see tangible evidence of your thought patterns and can work on transforming them to foster a more confident mindset.

Consistency and Evaluation

Maintaining a journal isn't just about documenting; it's about reflecting and acting upon the insights you uncover.

Staying on Track:

- **Schedule Check-Ins**: Set aside time weekly or monthly to go over your entries.

- **Identify Patterns**: Look for thought processes or events that consistently affect your self-confidence.

- **Set Goals**: Based on your insights, establish clear, achievable goals for personal growth.

Evaluating Your Progress:

- Ask yourself if you see improvement in your overall mood and self-perception.

- Notice if your responses to similar challenges have evolved.

- Celebrate the strides you've made in reshaping your thoughts and behaviors.

Real-Life Success Story:

Consider "Emma", who started journaling to cope with low self-esteem. By consistently logging her thoughts, she noticed a pattern of self-criticism linked to past academic failures. Through reflection, Emma replaced these negative thoughts with achievements she had overlooked and began to nurture her confidence.
Journaling is a powerful tool for self-discovery and can significantly impact your journey toward a more confident you. With diligence and an open heart, you can uncover and reshape your inner dialogue, laying the foundation for true and lasting self-confidence.

SETTING HEALTHY BOUNDARIES: THE CORNERSTONE OF SELF-RESPECT

The Science Behind It

Setting healthy boundaries is not about building walls; it's about bridging gaps in understanding ourselves and how we wish to be treated by others. It draws from the concept of self-determination in psychological theory. Studies show that individuals with clear personal boundaries tend to have higher self-esteem and are less vulnerable to stress and burnout.

• Research in the field of interpersonal relationships suggests that healthy boundaries can prevent emotional entanglement, which often leads to personal and professional conflicts.

• Cognitive behavioral theories highlight that setting boundaries can positively affect our thinking patterns, improving mental health and reducing anxiety.

• Neuroscience has linked the practice of setting boundaries to better emotional regulation, as the brain learns to recognize and communicate personal limits, reducing the likelihood of emotional overload.

Practical Implementation

To integrate healthy boundaries into your life, start by identifying what aspects you value most about yourself and your time. These steps can help:

1. **Self-Reflection**: Understand your limits by reflecting on past experiences. Which situations made you comfortable or uncomfortable, and why?

2. **Communicate Clearly**: Express your boundaries to others assertively and without apology. For example, "I value my family time on weekends, so I won't be available for work calls."

3. **Strategies for Enforcement**: Plan for how to maintain your boundaries. If someone asks you to do something that encroaches on your boundaries, have a polite but firm response ready.

4. **Practice Saying No**: It's a skill and like any other, it requires practice. Start with small, inconsequential requests, then work your way up.

5. **Self-Care**: Make sure that your own needs are met before trying to meet the needs of others.

Scenarios and Responses

- When asked to take on extra work that conflicts with personal time: "I appreciate your confidence in me, but I must decline due to prior commitments."

- If someone asks for a loan you're not comfortable giving: "I'm not in a position to lend money, but I can help in other ways if you need."

Consistency and Evaluation

It's crucial to consistently apply boundaries and to periodically evaluate their effectiveness.

- **Regular Assessment**: At set intervals (monthly, for example), review your boundaries to see if they are still serving you well.

- **Flexibility When Necessary**: Life circumstances change, and sometimes, so must our boundaries. Being adaptable can be just as important as setting the boundaries in the first place.

- **Self-Respect**: Remind yourself that boundaries are a sign of self-respect. Respect your own limits, and others will follow suit.

Remember that boundaries are not one-size-fits-all and what works for one person may not for another. Listen to your own needs and adjust as needed.

By following these practical steps and maintaining consistency, we teach others how we expect to be treated, which in turn solidifies our self-respect and enhances our confidence.

Real-Life Example: Julia, a web designer, made it a point to not answer work-related emails after 6 PM. Initially, there was some pushback from clients, but she held firm, explaining that this boundary allowed her to provide the best quality work during business hours. Over time, clients respected her time management, and she saw an improvement in both her work-life balance and client satisfaction.

CULTIVATING EMPATHY: THE CONNECTION BETWEEN CONFIDENCE AND COMPASSION

Empathy and confidence might seem like distinct aspects of our personalities, but they are more intertwined than we often realize. As we embark on this chapter, we shall unravel the subtle yet powerful links that bind these human traits, providing insight into how fostering empathy can not only enhance our ability to connect with others but also bolster our self-assurance and self-esteem.

The Science Behind It

Empathy, the ability to understand and share the feelings of others, is not just a moral compass; it's a social tool that is rooted in our biology. Research in the field of neuroscience has discovered that when people feel empathy, certain areas of the brain are activated – specifically, those associated with social awareness and emotional regulation. Empathy engages our neural networks, invoking a genuine understanding of others' perspectives.
From a psychological standpoint, empathic individuals often find themselves with a healthier self-image. When we practice empathy, we step outside of ourselves and this outward focus can reduce self-critique. Through this practice, a natural byproduct is a boost in our confidence as we realize our place in a broader social community and the value we can bring.

Key Points:

• Empathy activates brain regions linked to social cognition and emotional processing.

• It can minimize excessive self-focus and self-criticism, reinforcing a positive self-image.

• This outward focus extends our understanding of our social impact and personal efficacy.

Practical Implementation

Incorporating empathy into our daily lives and seeing it as a pathway to confidence requires purposeful action. Here, we detail steps to practice empathy actively and thus reap the related confidence rewards.

1. **Active Listening**: Begin by giving full attention to conversations, resisting the urge to formulate responses while others are speaking. This demands presence and a clear mind, allowing for deeper understanding of another's viewpoint.

2. **Body Language Awareness**: Non-verbal cues can communicate empathy. Nodding, maintaining eye contact, and turning your body towards someone show you value their interaction, which, in turn, can boost your own sense of self-worth.

3. **Challenge Prejudices**: Make a conscious effort to identify and challenge your biases. In considering other perspectives, you not only grow in empathy but also in self-knowledge, contributing to greater confidence.

4. **Ask Open-Ended Questions**: Encourage others to share more about their thoughts and feelings. This practice promotes a genuine interest in others, fostering connections and self-assurance in your communication skills.

Actionable Advice:

- Implement a "listening first" policy in discussions.

- Practice mirroring body language to show engagement.

- Keep a journal to reflect on biases and encounters with others.

Consistency and Evaluation

Like any skill, empathy requires regular practice and reflection for it to strengthen and have an impact on confidence. Setting aside time each day to engage empathetically and then analyzing those encounters can offer a clear gauge of progress.

1. **Set Empathy Goals**: Define what empathy looks like in daily interactions and strive to act accordingly. This could be as simple as having one heartfelt conversation per day.

2. **Reflect on Interactions**: At the end of each day, take a moment to reflect on conversations. Evaluate the quality of empathy displayed and how it felt, considering any changes in self-perception.

3. **Seek Feedback**: Engage with close friends or colleagues for honest feedback on your empathic behavior. Understanding how you are perceived can be a powerful motivator and confidence booster.

Steps for Consistency:

- Integrate empathic practices into daily routines.

- Reflect on empathetic interactions with a nightly journal entry.

- Request and act on feedback to improve empathic engagement.

In summary, empathy and confidence complement each other in a dance of personal growth that imbues our interactions with authenticity and warmth. By understanding the science, practically applying empathetic strategies, and regularly evaluating our progress, we can cultivate a deeply empathic and confident self, ready to connect and thrive in the complexities of our social world. As we conclude this chapter, remember that the journey to confidence is both an inward and outward adventure, enriched by the compassion we share and the connections we foster.

COMMUNICATION SKILLS: EXPRESSING YOURSELF WITH CLARITY AND CONFIDENCE

The Science Behind It

When we delve into the science of communication, we unearth a myriad of factors influencing how we express ourselves. Research spanning decades has identified key components that contribute to effective communication. These include:

- **Verbal cues**: The words we choose matter, but it is more about *how

- we say them. In fact, Albert Mehrabian's famous study concluded that the message we convey face-to-face is 7% verbal, 38% vocal (tone, inflection), and 55% nonverbal.

- **Non-verbal cues**: Our body language, eye contact, and gestures speak volumes even when we are silent. They can either reinforce our message or betray emotions we'd prefer to conceal.

- **Emotional Intelligence (EI)**: EI helps us understand and manage our emotions and those of others, thereby facilitating more effective communication.

- **Active listening**: Communication is a two-way street. Active listening involves fully concentrating on, understanding, responding to, and remembering what the other person says.

Understanding these components enables us to tweak our communication style to articulate thoughts more effectively, fostering both personal and professional growth.

Practical Implementation

To harness the power of the science and craft your own clear and confident communication style, follow these practical steps:

1. **Mind Your Language**: Choose words that convey your message clearly. Avoid jargon unless your audience is familiar with it. Use metaphors and similes to clarify complex ideas.

2. **Tone it Right**: Your tone can alter the message. Aim for a conversational, friendly yet respectful tone to make your audience feel at ease.

3. **Gestures and Posture**: Use open gestures and maintain good posture to appear confident. Mirroring the body language of your audience can also create a sense of rapport.

4. **Tame the Emotions**: Develop your EI by being aware of your emotions and learning techniques to manage them. This ensures your message isn't clouded by unintended emotional expression.

5. **Active Listening is Key**: Listen more than you speak. Acknowledge what has been said by summarizing it back to the speaker to affirm you've understood correctly.

6. **Continual Learning**: Familiarize yourself with communication strategies and continuously incorporate them into your daily interactions.

7. **Seek Feedback**: Ask your audience for feedback on your communication style to identify areas for improvement.

8. **Practice Makes Perfect**: Role-play various communication scenarios with a friend or mentor to build confidence in your ability to convey complex information simply and effectively.

Consistency and Evaluation

Maintaining consistency in effective communication is vital, but so is adaptability. As you grow more proficient, be prepared to adjust your approach to match the context and your audience. Regular evaluation of your progress helps to:

- Ensure you embody the principles of clear communication.

- Keep your skills sharp and up to date.

- Encourage reflexivity and mindfulness in interpersonal interactions.

Remember: Communication is an evolving field. Stay enlightened about new research and insights as they develop, and be ready to incorporate them into your practices.
And so, as you embark on your path to crystal-clear and confident communication, keep in mind the power of expressing yourself with precision. Embrace your unique voice, and allow your personal growth to shine through each word, gesture, and expression. Let this be not just a chapter in a book, but a transformative journey in your professional and personal life.

THE POWER OF ACTIVE LISTENING: BUILDING TRUST AND UNDERSTANDING

Listening is not merely hearing; it's an active process where attention is given to the speaker's words, emotions, and underlying message. It's the cornerstone of effective communication and thus plays a vital role in fostering confidence, self-esteem, and personal growth. In this chapter, we will delve into the mechanics of active listening, its practical application in our daily interactions, and methods for assessing its effectiveness.

The Science Behind It

When we engage in active listening, we are doing more than processing sound; we are interpreting, understanding, and developing empathy. Here's the science that makes this complex process invaluable:

- **Neural Mirroring**: Our brains have mirror neurons that help us empathize and understand what others feel, laying the groundwork for strong interpersonal relationships.

- **Memory Enhancement**: Active listening promotes better memory retention as it requires focus and engagement, imprinting the information more deeply in our minds.

- **Stress Reduction**: When we listen actively, we create smoother interactions that can reduce misunderstandings and conflicts, thus lowering stress levels for everyone involved.

- **Emotional Intelligence**: Through active listening, we become adept at reading between the lines, recognizing the speaker's emotions, which is fundamental to emotional intelligence.

Practical Implementation

Now, let's put active listening into practice. Here are some strategies that we can incorporate into our daily interactions to improve our relationships and bolster confidence:

1. **Maintain Eye Contact**: This shows the speaker they have your undivided attention.

2. **Nod and Smile**: Nonverbal cues let the speaker know you're with them and can encourage more open communication.

3. **Rephrase Content**: Reflect on what's been said by paraphrasing. It demonstrates your understanding and gives the speaker a chance to clarify.

4. **Be Present**: Avoid distractions. Give the speaker the gift of your full presence.

5. **Ask Probing Questions**: Inquire for detail or clarification. This shows your interest and deepens your understanding.

To illustrate, consider Sarah, a project manager who realized her team's productivity was slipping. Instead of sending another email, she organized one-on-one meetings, listening intently to her team members' concerns and suggestions. By applying active listening, she gained insights into the challenges they faced and made everyone feel valued and understood. The result? A rejuvenated team and improved project outcomes.

Consistency and Evaluation

Like any skill, active listening requires practice and consistency. Here are some pointers for ensuring you make active listening a natural part of your interactions:

- **Set Listening Goals**: For the next team meeting or one-on-one, set an intention to listen deeply, even if the subject doesn't naturally pique your interest.

- **Reflect on Interactions**: After conversations, take a moment to consider how effectively you listened. What could you have understood better?

- **Seek Feedback**: Ask colleagues or friends for their honest opinion on your listening skills. They might offer valuable insights into areas for improvement.

Evaluation can come in many forms, from self-assessment to feedback from others. Additionally, consider the qualitative changes in your relationships—are they growing stronger? Is there a noticeable increase in trust? These are good indicators of effective active listening.

In conclusion, remember that active listening is not an innate talent, but a skill that can be honed. By practicing and evaluating your active listening abilities, you can build trust, improve understanding, and enhance your overall personal growth. This chapter has outlined the science, practical implementation, and methods for assessment; now take these tools and integrate them into your path of developing confidence and self-esteem. Happy listening!

ASKING FOR HELP: STRENGTH IN VULNERABILITY

In a world that often prizes self-reliance and individual prowess, it can be daunting to acknowledge our need for assistance. Yet, in this chapter, we'll explore how asking for help is not a sign of weakness but rather an emblem of strength and a pivotal step in personal growth. Embracing vulnerability is a courageous act that can facilitate confidence and self-esteem, thereby enriching our path to personal transformation.

The Science Behind It

- **Neurological Perspective:**

  - Studies show that social support can activate the brain's reward system, making the act of seeking help not just emotionally beneficial but also neurologically rewarding.

  - Vulnerability can lead to stronger connections with others, as it fosters empathy and trust—key components in lasting relationships.

- **Psychological Benefits:**

  ○ Psychologists find that individuals who are open to asking for help often have higher self-esteem, as they recognize their worth and the value of their goals, prompting them to leverage available resources.

  ○ Vulnerability and the willingness to seek support can be linked to greater resilience; facing challenges with others' aid helps us learn how to adapt and overcome obstacles more effectively.

Practical Implementation

To seamlessly integrate the act of asking for help into your life, consider the following strategies:

1. **Reframe Your Perception:**

   ○ Start by reframing your perception of help-seeking as a proactive and strategic decision rather than a last-resort measure.

2. **Identify Needs:**

   ○ Clearly identify the areas in which you require assistance, thus making your requests for help targeted and effective.

3. **Choose the Right People:**

   ○ Assess who in your network possesses the skills or experience relevant to your needs, increasing the chance of beneficial outcomes.

4. **Communicate Clearly and Specifically:**

   ○ When asking for help, be clear and specific about what you need. This helps others understand your request and improves the chance of a positive response.

5. **Express Gratitude:**

   ◦ Always express gratitude for the help received. It fosters goodwill and encourages continued support.

6. **Be Reciprocal:**

   ◦ Offer help to others when you can. This builds a culture of mutual support and strengthens relationships.

Consistency and Evaluation

- **Regular Practice:**

   ◦ Like any skill, regularly practicing vulnerability and asking for help makes it more natural. Set small weekly goals to reach out for assistance in areas you would normally avoid.

- **Evaluate Outcomes:**

   ◦ Reflect on occasions where you asked for help. Evaluate the outcomes and how they contributed to personal growth.

- **Adjust Strategies:**

   ◦ If an approach does not yield expected results, reassess and adjust your methods. Perhaps a different communication style or support network would yield better outcomes.

Illustration:

Consider *Samantha*, a young entrepreneur who rarely asked for help, fearing it would undermine her authority. However, after mentoring, she started to solicit input from her team more frequently. This openness not only improved her business's strategic decisions but also fostered a more collaborative and confident team.

In conclusion, the act of asking for help signifies a secure awareness of our capacities and the discernment to amplify our potential with the strengths of others. It's a courageous endeavor that feeds confidence and signals a sophisticated level of emotional intelligence vital for personal and professional development. As we consistently practice this subtle art, our self-esteem evolves and our journey to 'a new you' becomes deeply enriched.

NAVIGATING CONFLICT WITH CONFIDENCE: STRATEGIES FOR A POSITIVE OUTCOME

The Science Behind It

Conflict is an inevitable part of life, but it's our response to it that shapes the outcome. While the instinctive 'fight or flight' reaction to conflict is etched deeply in our brain's amygdala, modern science advocates for a more thoughtful approach that engages our prefrontal cortex, the area responsible for complex behaviors and decision making.

- **Psychology of Perceptions:** Conflicts often arise from differing perceptions. Awareness of cognitive biases and the fundamental attribution error—where we attribute others' behaviors to their character but our own to the situation—can help us navigate conflict more effectively.

- **Stress Response Management:** Physical reactions to stress can short-circuit rational thinking. Techniques like deep breathing and mindfulness can help maintain calm, allowing us to engage constructively.

- **Effective Communication Theories:** Models like Nonviolent Communication (NVC) help identify emotional states and needs, fostering empathy and collaborative problem-solving.

Practical Implementation

Incorporating the science into everyday conflict situations involves deliberate practice and communication tactics.

1. **Active Listening:** Show genuine interest in understanding the other person's point of view without interrupting or planning your rebuttal.

2. **Emotional Intelligence:** Recognize your emotions and their origin. Acknowledge the feelings of everyone involved without judgment.

3. **I-Statements:** Frame your message around how you feel rather than accusing the other person, which can reduce defensiveness.

4. **Seek Win-Win Solutions:** Aim for outcomes that address the needs of all parties. This could mean compromising or inventing creative solutions that satisfy everyone.

Example: During a miscommunication at work, instead of saying "You never listen to my ideas," try "I feel my contributions aren't taken into consideration. How can we improve this?"

Consistency and Evaluation

Transforming how we handle conflict is not a one-off task but a continuous journey that requires reflection and adjustment.

- Develop a **routine check-in** with yourself after conflicts to analyze what went well and what could be better.

- Keep a conflict **resolution journal** where you can track patterns in the conflicts you're involved in and your responses to them.

- Solicit **feedback** from trusted peers or mentors on your conflict resolution skills.

Remember, confidence in conflict doesn't mean you always 'win'. It means navigating disagreements assertively and constructively, building stronger relationships and self-respect in the process. Maintain balance and objectivity throughout the chapter, and avoid making sweeping generalizations. Each conflict is unique and requires a tailored response.

THE INFLUENCE OF SOCIAL CIRCLES: CHOOSING RELATIONSHIPS THAT EMPOWER YOU

The Science Behind It

When we talk about social circles, we're referring to the various groupings of people with whom we interact — friends, family, colleagues, and acquaintances. These groups have a profound impact on our confidence and self-esteem.

- **Mirror Neurons**: Our brains contain mirror neurons that help us understand and reflect the emotions and actions of those around us. When we surround ourselves with positive, confident individuals, it encourages us to emulate those attitudes.

- **Social Comparison Theory**: We intuitively measure ourselves against others. In a supportive environment, these comparisons can inspire growth rather than fostering feelings of inadequacy.

- **Emotional Contagion**: Emotions can be contagious. Encouraging relationships foster an atmosphere where confidence breeds confidence.

Real-World Example: Consider a study group in college. When the group is composed of motivated students, members are more likely to adopt similar habits and mindsets, leading to better performance in their courses.

Practical Implementation

Transforming your social circles might not happen overnight, but with intentional effort, you can steer your relationships in a direction that bolsters your self-esteem and confidence.

1. **Audit Your Circle**: Take stock of the people you spend the most time with. Are they positive influences? Do they support your goals and celebrate your successes?

2. **Seek Inspiring Company**: Join clubs, groups, or online communities where you can meet people who share your aspirations and who might serve as role models.

3. **Set Boundaries**: Don't be afraid to set boundaries with people who drain your energy or undermine your confidence. It's okay to say no to negativity.

4. **Cultivate Relationships**: Invest time in relationships with people who encourage you. These connections will become a reliable source of support and motivation.

Illustration: Imagine your social circle as a garden. As you prune back the overgrown, life-sapping weeds, you make room to plant new seeds — relationships that will flourish and, in turn, help you to do the same.

Consistency and Evaluation

Maintaining a empowering social circle requires regular attention and assessment. Here's how:

• **Monthly Check-Ins**: Reflect on your interactions and feelings after spending time with various people in your circle.

• **Quality over Quantity**: Focus on nurturing deeper connections with fewer people, rather than spreading yourself thin across many superficial relationships.

• **Seek Feedback**: Ask for input from trusted friends or mentors about how they perceive your interactions within your social groups.

Remember, cultivating a supportive social circle is a dynamic process. It evolves as you do, so regular evaluation is crucial. By consciously curating the individuals in your life, you can create an empowering ecosystem that nurtures your confidence and fosters personal growth. After all, we're social creatures, and the company we keep not only reflects who we are but also helps shape who we become.

REFRAMING FAILURE: LESSONS LEARNED FROM SETBACKS

The Science Behind It

Failure can stir up feelings of disappointment, embarrassment, and discouragement. However, from a psychological perspective, it can also be a powerful catalyst for growth and learning. The concept of a "growth mindset," popularized by psychologist Carol Dweck, suggests that individuals who see failure as an opportunity to grow are more likely to achieve success in the long run. This mindset frames setbacks not as insurmountable obstacles but as stepping stones to mastery.
Research indicates that when we fail, various cognitive and emotional processes occur that, if harnessed correctly, can lead to enhanced problem-solving abilities and resilience. Neurally, failure triggers the brain to pay closer attention and process information more deeply – this is our natural learning response.

- Our brains evaluate and analyze what went wrong.

- We experience increased retention of the lessons learned, thanks to the emotional salience of our mistakes.

- We are prompted to revise our strategies and approach problems from different angles.

By embracing failure as a natural part of the learning process, we can begin to shed the fear of it, enhance our confidence, and approach challenges with renewed vigor.

Practical Implementation

To harness the constructive power of setbacks, we can implement various strategies:

1. **Mindfulness and Reflection**: Take a moment to reflect on what happened without judgment. Mindfulness can help you observe the situation from a distance, reducing the sting of failure and allowing you to analyze it objectively.

2. **Constructive Feedback Loop**: Build a support system that offers constructive feedback. Whether it's a mentor or a peer group, having others help you assess your failures can provide new perspectives and insights.

3. **Adjust and Act**: Based on your reflections and the feedback received, make necessary adjustments to your approach. This might mean honing a particular skill, shifting your strategy, or simply trying again with a better understanding of the potential pitfalls.

4. **Set Small, Achievable Goals**: Break down your larger goals into smaller, manageable steps. Achieving these smaller goals will build confidence and provide a clear path forward, making the next setback less intimidating.

Remember, the key isn't to avoid failure, but to learn how to respond to it constructively.

Consistency and Evaluation

Maintaining a consistent approach to dealing with setbacks is key to transforming how you handle failure. This doesn't mean that you won't feel the sting of disappointment, but rather that you're committed to responding to failure in a way that promotes learning and growth. Regularly evaluating your responses to failures will help you refine your approach over time.

- **Keep a Failure Journal**: Documenting your setbacks and your responses to them can be incredibly enlightening. Over time, you'll be able to see patterns in how you handle failure and learn from them.

- **Celebrate the Lessons**: Instead of celebrating only successes, try celebrating the lessons learned from each failure. This can help shift your mindset to one that values progress and personal growth.

- **Revisit and Revise**: Your approach to failure should evolve as you do. Periodically revisit your strategies for dealing with setbacks to ensure they still align with your goals and growth.

By consistently practicing these strategies, you turn failure from a dreaded outcome into a constructive tool in your personal development arsenal. The confidence and self-esteem gained through overcoming setbacks are often more substantial and enduring than those built on unchallenged successes.

In conclusion, as we learn to reframe our failures as opportunities for growth, we build resilience, confidence, and a foundation for long-term personal success. Each setback teaches us a new lesson about our capabilities and how we can transcend our perceived limitations. Embrace each challenge with an open mind, and let your journey be a story of continuous learning and triumph over adversity.

OVERCOMING PERFECTIONISM: EMBRACING 'GOOD ENOUGH'

The Science Behind It

Perfectionism isn't just a personal quirk; it's a psychological construct with both benefits and drawbacks. While striving for perfection can drive quality and improvement, when it spirals out of control, it can lead to increased stress, anxiety, and even paralysis of action. The science tells us that adaptive perfectionists achieve high standards without suffering as much from the negative effects, while maladaptive perfectionists are never quite satisfied, leading to burnout and mental health issues.

Neuroscientific studies suggest that perfectionism is linked to brain activity patterns, particularly in areas related to error processing and self-reflection. When our brain perpetually signals that nothing is ever good enough, we end up in a circuit of perpetual dissatisfaction. Behavioral psychology points out that perfectionism can be a learned trait, reinforced by societal expectations.

Understanding this is crucial to embracing 'good enough'. Research tells us that aiming for 'good enough' can:

- Enhance creativity by lowering the fear of failure.

- Increase productivity by reducing the time spent on diminishing returns.

- Improve mental health by relieving the pressure associated with perfection.

- Foster a growth mindset, which values progress over outcome.

Practical Implementation

To cultivate a 'good enough' mindset, consider the following actionable steps:

1. **Set Realistic Goals**: Identify what's truly important and recognize that imperfection does not equate to failure. Align your goals with realistic standards and timelines.

2. **Reframe Thoughts**: Challenge perfectionist thinking by asking yourself if your standards are truly necessary. Could 'good enough' work just as well?

3. **Prioritize Tasks**: Focus on the most impact-generating tasks first. By prioritizing, you can ensure quality where it matters most, while being more flexible with lesser tasks.

4. **Embrace Mistakes**: See mistakes as learning opportunities. Understand that the path to excellence is paved with errors and that each one teaches you something valuable.

5. **Practice Self-Compassion**: Treat yourself with the kindness you would offer others. Understand that being human means being inherently flawed and that's okay.

6. **Limit the Scope**: Reduce the breadth of your projects. By narrowing your focus, you can channel your efforts more effectively without spreading yourself too thin.

7. **Set Time Limits**: Impose deadlines for decisions and tasks. This can help prevent overthinking and encourage you to accept 'good enough' in a timeframe.

These steps, when consistently applied, will help you shift from a perfectionist mindset to one that values progress and the beauty of 'good enough'.

Consistency and Evaluation

Adopting a 'good enough' approach requires consistent practice and evaluation. Track your progress with the following methods:

- **Keep a Journal**: Write down instances where 'good enough' benefited you, noting how it felt and the outcomes it produced.

- **Seek Feedback**: Get outside perspectives on your work to gauge if additional effort would significantly change the outcome.

- **Set Review Points**: Choose intervals to review your work and assess whether striving for perfection made a quantifiable difference.

Remember: It's about finding balance. Some tasks may require a closer step towards perfection, while others will thrive with the 'good enough' principle. Regularly check in with yourself to make sure you're not slipping back into old habits.

Perfectionism is a tough habit to break, but with intentional action and consistent self-evaluation, you can learn to embrace the liberating concept of 'good enough.' This chapter aims not to discourage high standards but to advocate for a healthier, more balanced route to achieving them—one that boosts your confidence and allows personal growth without the crippling weight of impossible ideals.

CONFRONTING FEARS: THE ROLE OF COURAGE IN CONFIDENCE

The Science Behind It

The interplay between courage and confidence is a subject of much interest in psychological research. Courage, by its nature, implies a willingness to face fear and difficulty, and its cultivation can lead to increased self-esteem and confidence over time. The science suggests a virtuous cycle: as we act with courage, our confidence grows, and as our confidence grows, it becomes easier to act with courage.

- **Neuroscience**: When we confront our fears, the amygdala – the brain's fear center – activates. However, repeated courageous behaviors can rewire the neural pathways, leading to less fear and more confidence.

- **Biochemistry**: Courageous acts typically involve stress, which triggers the release of adrenaline. Learning to manage this stress response can build self-assurance.

- **Behavioral Psychology**: Positive reinforcement of courageous acts (e.g., succeeding in a task) naturally increases the likelihood of engaging in similar behaviors in the future, thus steadily building confidence.

Practical Implementation

To apply the principles from the science of courage and confidence, consider these strategies:

1. **Start Small**: Begin with low-risk situations that challenge you mildly and build up to more challenging scenarios.

2. **Visualization**: Picture yourself successfully navigating a situation that requires courage, which can decrease anxiety and increase the likelihood of success.

3. **Power Posing**: Adopting a powerful stance can actually result in psychological and physiological changes that enhance confidence.

Real-Life Examples:

• **Public Speaking**: Start by speaking in front of a small, supportive group before tackling larger audiences.

• **Network Building**: Begin with one-on-one meetings before going to larger networking events.

Consistency and Evaluation

Developing courage and consequently confidence requires consistent action and reflection:

• **Maintain a Courage Journal**: Document your acts of courage, however big or small, and reflect on the outcomes as well as your internal response.

• **Set Courage Goals**: Have weekly objectives that involve stepping out of your comfort zone.

- **Evaluate Progress**: Set aside time regularly to assess your growth in confidence. Recognize patterns in what works for you and what doesn't.

Remember, courage isn't the absence of fear—it's the triumph over it. Your confidence grows every time you confront a fear and come out the other side. Let each act of courage serve as proof that you are capable of more than you might currently believe. Keep pushing the boundaries, and watch as your confidence soars.

MANAGING ANXIETY: TECHNIQUES FOR STAYING CALM AND COLLECTED

In the journey toward personal growth and boosted confidence, managing anxiety is akin to clearing the path of obstacles. It's about equipping yourself with the tools to navigate through the inevitable bouts of uncertainty life throws your way. So, let's embark on an exploration of tranquility techniques designed to usher you into a state of calm and collected poise.

The Science Behind It

Anxiety isn't merely a feeling; it's a complex neurochemical symphony. When your brain perceives a threat—real or imagined—it sounds the alarm, releasing a cascade of hormones like adrenaline and cortisol. It's our built-in "fight or flight" mechanism, harkening back to ancestral days when physical danger was a more commonplace.

- *Neuroplasticity*: Our brains can literally reshape themselves through our thoughts and behaviors. Positive, calming practices can foster neural pathways that make tranquility more accessible.

- *Mind-Body Connection*: The vagus nerve serves as a communication highway between your brain and many internal organs. Techniques that stimulate this nerve, like deep breathing, promote relaxation.

• *Hormonal Influences*: Activities that increase 'feel-good' hormones, like serotonin and oxytocin, can combat stress hormones and mitigate anxiety.

Now, with the underlying science as our blueprint, let's delve into how you can infuse this knowledge into your daily routine.

Practical Implementation

To manage anxiety, you need a toolkit—practical, easy-to-implement strategies that can withstand the rigors of real life. Let's stock that toolkit now.

1. **Mindful Breathing**:

    ◦ **Diaphragmatic Breathing**: Practice taking slow, deep breaths that expand your diaphragm, which can turn down the dial on your sympathetic nervous system.

    ◦ **4-7-8 Technique**: Inhale for 4 seconds, hold for 7, and exhale for

2. It's like a reset button for a frazzled mind.

3. **Guided Visualization**:

    ◦ Imagine a serene environment. Use all your senses to make it as vivid as possible. This can help withdraw your mind from stress triggers.

4. **Progressive Muscle Relaxation**:

    ◦ Tense each muscle group for a few seconds then release. It's like giving anxiety a one-two punch, physically and mentally.

5. **Cognitive Behavioral Techniques**:

   ◦ Challenge and reframe negative thoughts. Replace "I can't handle this" with "I've handled tough situations before, I can do it again".

6. **Lifestyle Choices**:

   ◦ Regular exercise, a well-balanced diet, and adequate sleep are the pillars holding up your anti-anxiety fortress.

7. **Joyful Activities**:

   ◦ Engage in hobbies and passions. These not only distract but also create a stream of positive experiences and emotions to draw from.

Remember, Clara, the busy project manager who beat meeting anxiety by pictorially re-scripting her audience in whimsical attire? Or Mike, the coder who overcame deadline dread with a pre-work ritual featuring his favorite kooky dance playlist? Real people, real results.

Consistency and Evaluation

The golden thread that ties these techniques together isn't just knowledge—it's consistent practice. Anxiety doesn't dissipate after a one-off effort; it requires a steadfast approach, much like building muscle at the gym.

• **Routine**: Integrate these strategies into your daily routine. Make it as habitual as your morning cup of coffee.

• **Journaling**: Track your progress and feelings in a journal. This reflexivity can provide insights into what works best for you.

• **Adaptation**: Be prepared to adapt your strategy. If after a few weeks one technique isn't serving you, pivot to another.

- **Support**: Engage with a community or seek support from a professional. You don't have to manage anxiety in isolation.

In summary, managing anxiety is a journey of understanding its mechanics, adopting practical strategies, and committing to consistent practice and evaluation. With each step, you fortify your confidence, building a more serene, unshakeable foundation for personal growth. Remember, managing anxiety isn't about erasing it; it's about mastering the art of staying calm and collected amidst life's symphony.

RESILIENCE: GETTING BACK UP AFTER A FALL

The Science Behind It

Resilience, often illustrated as the psychological "bouncing back" muscle, signifies the capacity to recover from adversities, whether they be personal mistakes, professional setbacks, or life's random curveballs. Research in positive psychology has demystified the idea that resilience is a congenital trait, shining a light on it as a buildable skill.

- **The Resilient Brain**: Neuroplasticity is our brain's ability to adapt and rewire itself. Each time we encounter a challenge and actively work through it, we're not just 'getting past it', we're fundamentally conditioning our neural circuits to handle stress more efficiently next time.

- **Emotional Regulation**: Resilient individuals harness the power of emotions such as optimism and perspective. They aren't immune to feelings of anxiety or depression, but they've practiced managing their emotions in a way that facilitates recovery.

- **Supportive Relationships**: The influence of a robust social network cannot be overstated. Studies have repeatedly shown that having strong, supportive relationships bolsters our resilience.

Understanding the science helps dismantle the myth of the "naturally resilient" and underscores the fact that everyone can foster this fortitude through consistent practice and mindset shifts.

Practical Implementation

Transforming knowledge into action is where most people fumble. It's simple to talk about the mechanics of resilience, but quite another to cultivate it.

1. **Self-Awareness Exercises**: Log your responses to stress. What triggers you? How do you react, both physically and emotionally?

2. **Mindfulness and Relaxation**: Integrating mindfulness practices into your daily routine can help ground you in the present and reduce anxiety.

3. **Positive Affirmations**: Cultivate a positive inner dialogue. Remind yourself of your strengths and achievements with regular affirmations.

4. **Problem-Solving Skills**: Rather than avoiding challenging tasks, face them head-on. This strengthens your belief in your own abilities.

5. **Seek Challenges**: Step outside your comfort zone. Small, manageable challenges can help build confidence and resilience.

The objective is not to shield oneself from failures or difficulties but to develop a toolkit that helps navigate through them with grace and tenacity.

Consistency and Evaluation

Like any skill, resilience requires regular conditioning. It isn't about a single monumental bounce-back; it's about how we integrate our responses to setbacks into our daily life.

- **Daily Reflection**: At the day's end, reflect on how you confronted challenges. What worked? What didn't?

- **Adjustment of Tactics**: Use failures as feedback. If a particular approach to a problem didn't pan out, change your strategy.

- **Measure Progress**: Set benchmarks for yourself. Celebrating small victories is crucial for maintaining motivation and perspective on your journey.

Evaluation isn't just about noting what you could've done better; it's about recognizing the strides you've made in strengthening your resilience and giving yourself credit where it's due. Throughout this chapter, we've explored the components that underpin resilience. From understanding its scientific foundations to practical everyday applications and consistent review, we can turn setbacks into setups for future successes. The essence of resilience lies in the perpetual quest not just to withstand the storm but to learn to dance in the rain.

TAKING RISKS: CALCULATED CHANCES FOR PERSONAL GROWTH

In the pursuit of personal growth, there's an old adage that still resonates under our modern spotlight: "No risk, no reward." Breaking down the elements of risk-taking, this chapter will delve into harnessing its power for confidence building and self-improvement, steering clear from reckless leaps and focusing on the strategic gambles that can lead to profound growth.

The Science Behind It

Risk-taking is wired into our psyche; it's a fundamental aspect of our evolutionary history. Our ancestors who took calculated risks —like venturing into unknown territories to find food or seeking new shelter—often reaped rewards critical for survival.

• **Psychological Benefits**: When we embrace risk responsibly, our brain releases dopamine, a neurotransmitter associated with pleasure and reward. This effect can lead to a heightened sense of accomplishment and confidence.

• **Growth Mindset**: Studies in neuroscience show that challenging ourselves with new tasks can help foster a growth mindset, leading to neuroplasticity – the brain's ability to change and adapt through experience.

• **Resilience**: Each risk taken and overcome increases our resilience, providing a feedback loop that enhances our ability to handle failure and unpredictability.

Taking risks is a balancing act—too little, and we stagnate, too much, and we could encounter unnecessary hardship. The key is calculated risk-taking, a methodical approach where the potential benefits are weighed against the possible costs.

Practical Implementation

To translate the science of risk-taking to daily life, consider the following steps:

1. **Risk Assessment**: Before embarking on any venture, take a moment to assess the potential outcomes. List the pros and cons, and seek advice if needed. This helps ensure that the risks taken are calculated, not haphazard.

2. **Start Small**: Begin with low-stakes risks to build your confidence. This might mean speaking up in a meeting or trying a new hobby. Success in these areas can embolden you for bigger challenges.

3. **Preparation**: Gather as much information and skill as possible related to your risk. The more prepared you are, the less daunting the risk becomes.

4. **Set Measurable Goals**: Have clear, attainable goals for your risk-taking endeavors. This will provide a sense of direction and a way to track progress.

5. **Reflect on Past Success**: Remember times in the past when taking a risk led to a positive outcome. This can motivate and bolster your self-assurance.

Consistency and Evaluation

Maintaining a consistent approach to risk-taking is vital. Here's how you can make it a regular part of your journey towards personal growth:

- Make it a habit to step outside of your comfort zone regularly.

- Regularly review the outcomes of your risks, adjust your strategy based on what you've learned.

- Celebrate wins, but also view losses as lessons. Each experience provides invaluable insights for future risks.

Consistent Efforts:

- Weekly Challenges: Set yourself a new challenge each week that requires some level of risk.

- Learning Journal: Keep a journal of risks taken, the results, and lessons learned to track your growth.

Regular Evaluation:

- Monthly Reflections: At the end of each month, reflect on the risks you've taken. What has worked? What hasn't?

- Feedback Loop: Seek feedback from trusted friends, family, or mentors to gain perspective on your risk-taking journey.

Engaging Examples

Consider the story of Sarah, who decided to change her career at 30. Calculating the risks, she went back to school while working part-time and emerged with a degree that led to her dream job. Or Jake, who overcame his fear of public speaking by joining a local speaking club, paving the way for career advancement.

Both cases illustrate the potential for personal and professional growth when calculated risks are taken. Each small victory bolstered their confidence, constructing a sturdier foundation for even greater aspirations.

In conclusion, taking risks is not about throwing caution to the wind, but about mindful exploration—expanding your horizons in measured steps. With each calculated chance, you pave the way for new opportunities, experiences, and a more confident you. In this realm of possibility, personal growth is not just a hopeful outcome; it's practically inevitable.

LETTING GO OF WHAT DOESN'T SERVE YOU: MOVING FORWARD WITH PURPOSE

In our journey toward confidence and personal growth, we often encounter obstacles that prevent us from reaching our full potential. Sometimes, these barriers are external, but often, they are created by our own habits and thought patterns that no longer serve us. This chapter aims to help you identify what's holding you back, understand the science of letting go, and provide practical steps towards moving forward purposefully and confidently.

The Science Behind It

The human brain is remarkably adaptable, but it also has a tendency to cling to familiar patterns—even those that are detrimental to our well-being. This is due, in part, to a concept called the "status quo bias," where individuals prefer things to remain the same by doing nothing or by sticking with a decision made previously.

On the other side of the spectrum, neuroscience demonstrates that our brains have the capacity for 'neuroplasticity'—the ability to form new connections and pathways. This adaptability is the key to letting go of what doesn't serve us. By consciously focusing on new, constructive thoughts and behaviors, we can rewire our brains and foster positive changes in our lives.

- Neuroscientists believe it takes approximately 66 days for a new behavior to become automatic.

- Emotional attachment to past experiences can create a comfort zone, acting as a barrier to letting go.

- Mindfulness and reflection practices are shown to decrease the stress associated with change, thus aiding the letting-go process.

Practical Implementation

The process of letting go can be challenging but rewarding. Here are practical steps you can adopt on your journey:

1. **Reflection**: Invest time in identifying the thought patterns, relationships, or habits that are holding you back. Write them down and be honest with yourself.

2. **Decision**: Make a conscious decision to change. Without this step, the cycle of clinging to the unhelpful will continue.

3. **Small Steps**: Start with small, manageable changes rather than broad, sweeping ones. This could mean setting aside ten minutes a day for a new hobby that builds confidence or practicing positive self-talk every morning.

4. **Support System**: Surround yourself with a network of support, whether it be friends, family, or colleagues who encourage your growth.

5. **Adaptation**: Stay flexible and willing to adapt your strategies as you discover what works best for you.

6. Establish clear, achievable goals related to letting go and building confidence.

7. Use visualization techniques to imagine life without the burdens you're shedding.

8. Develop a 'letting go' ritual or practice that signals your commitment to this process.

Consistency and Evaluation

Like building any skill, letting go requires consistent effort and periodic evaluation.

- **Daily Reminders**: Leave yourself notes, set alarms, or use apps to keep your goals at the forefront of your daily life.

- **Tracking Progress**: Keep a journal of your journey—note feelings, setbacks, and victories.

- **Regular Review**: Schedule a time each week to reflect on what strategies are working and what needs adjustment.

Through this consistent and evaluative approach, you can make steady progress towards freeing yourself from what doesn't serve you and fostering the confidence necessary for personal growth. Letting go is not an easy task—it is a complex process that involves introspection, commitment, and resilience. The liberation that comes from releasing those unproductive elements, however, can be the catalyst for a life filled with greater confidence, self-esteem, and fulfillment. As you move forward with purpose, remember that letting go is not just about loss; it's about creating space for new opportunities and experiences that align with your best self.

GOAL SETTING: MAPPING OUT YOUR CONFIDENCE JOURNEY

In the grand adventure of self-improvement, setting clear and precise goals is like charting a course for a ship on open seas. Confidence is not a destination that you stumble upon accidentally; it is a journey that requires intention, direction, and commitment. So, let's embark together on this voyage, using the stars of science and the compass of practical application to navigate towards our treasure—unwavering self-confidence.

The Science Behind It

Recent advancements in psychology have illuminated how setting goals activates our inner potential and fuels our self-confidence. When we set goals:

- **Our Brain's Role:**

  - Neurologically, goals give our brain a clear focus. Our reticular activating system (RAS) helps filter unnecessary information and directs our attention to what's important—our objectives.

  - Dopamine, the 'feel-good' neurotransmitter, is released not just when we achieve goals, but also when we make progress towards them, reinforcing our motivation and confidence.

- **SMART Goals:**

  - Specific, Measurable, Achievable, Relevant, and Time-bound (SMART) goals are the blueprint of success. They provide a framework that puts the vast abstract of confidence into concrete chunks that can be tackled.

- **Visualization and Confidence:**

  - Visualizing achieving our goals has shown to forge paths in our brains, creating a mental model of our desired outcome that enhances our belief in our ability to succeed.

- **The Power of Incremental Success:**

  - Smaller milestones within larger goals help to build what's called 'self-efficacy', the belief in our capabilities to execute the necessary actions to achieve specific performances.

Practical Implementation

Let's translate the above science into actionable steps. Like a gardener nurturing a seed, you must tend to the following practices regularly to grow the plant of confidence.

- **Define Your Confidence Goals:**

  1. Imagine what confidence looks like for you. Is it speaking up in meetings, making new friends, or perhaps public speaking?

  2. Use the SMART criteria to set goals that align with your confidence vision.

- **Break Down Your Goals:**

  1. Slice your objectives into smaller, manageable tasks—this will make your journey less daunting.

  2. Celebrate every small victory, as this increases self-efficacy and thus confidence.

- **Create a Confidence Journal:**

  ○ Track your progress, reflect on what works, and adjust your approach as necessary. This is your logbook on the high seas of self-improvement.

- **Find a Role Model or Mentor:**

  ○ Learning from others' journeys can offer guidance, motivate you, and bolster your belief in your capacity to achieve your goals.

- **Practice Mindfulness and Positive Affirmations:**

  ○ Incorporate daily meditations or affirmations that keep you anchored to your goals and resilient against the waves of doubt.

Consistency and Evaluation

Like the ongoing effort to navigate by maintaining a ship's course, you must remain diligent in your pursuit of confidence.

- **Regular Check-Ins:**

  ○ Schedule weekly or monthly evaluations of your progress.

  ○ Adapt your methods and goals as needed, using your experiences as learning opportunities.

- **Patience is Key:**

  - Remember that confidence-building is a gradual process. Frustration and setbacks are part of any worthy expedition.

- **Seek Feedback:**

  - Don't sail the journey alone; seek constructive feedback from trusted mates to help refine your strategies.

- **Accountability Partners:**

  - An accountability buddy can keep you on track—two compasses are better than one when ensuring you're heading in the right direction.

In summary, setting definitive, practical goals and consistently evaluating your progress will map out a clear path to heightened self-confidence. By understanding the science, putting it into practice, and maintaining a resilient and adaptable approach, your confidence will not just bloom—it will flourish. Anchors aweigh to uncharted waters, for your confidence journey awaits!

TIME MANAGEMENT: PRIORITIZING PERSONAL DEVELOPMENT

The Science Behind It

Personal development is an integral component in the quest to boost confidence and self-esteem. Research unequivocally supports the notion that individuals who engage regularly in self-improvement activities tend to display higher levels of self-assurance and contentment in their personal and professional lives. Psychologists argue that the act of setting aside time for personal development is conducive to goal attainment, which in turn, fuels confidence. Essentially, the process plays upon the principles of self-efficacy — the belief in one's ability to succeed. When we consistently meet the small goals set out in personal development plans, our sense of self-efficacy is fortified, leading to greater overall confidence.

Moreover, neuroscientific studies reveal that learning new skills and adapting to new routines can enhance neural plasticity. This adaptability is the brain's capacity to rewire itself, which isn't just pivotal for learning and memory but also for cultivating resilience and a positive self-image.

Practical Implementation

Embarking on the journey of personal development requires strategic planning coupled with actionable steps. Here's a streamlined approach to get you started:

1. **Set SMART Goals**:

   - *Specific*: Define what area of personal development you wish to focus on.

   - *Measurable*: Ensure you can track your progress.

   - *Achievable*: Set realistic expectations.

   - *Relevant*: Choose goals that align with your long-term objectives.

   - *Time-bound*: Set a deadline to maintain urgency.

2. **Create a Personal Development Plan (PDP)**:

   - Outline the skills or qualities you desire to cultivate or enhance.

   - Identify resources you need — books, courses, mentors.

   - Allocate specific time slots in your week dedicated to this growth.

3. **Apply the 80/20 Rule**:

   - Focus on the 20% of activities that will yield 80% of your personal development results. This could mean honing a key skill that will dramatically improve your confidence.

4. **Establish a Routine**:

   - Integrate personal development into your daily routine. This might mean starting your morning with a meditation or educational podcast.

5. **Monitor Your Energy Levels**:

   ○ Capitalize on when you are most alert and focused to tackle tasks that demand high cognitive effort.

By adhering to this practical framework, you'll craft a pathway that not only nurtures your personal growth but does so efficiently and effectively.

Consistency and Evaluation

Sustained growth and confidence are not the results of sporadic efforts but of persistent dedication and periodic assessment.

- **Daily Habits**:

   ○ Incorporate small, daily habits that build upon each other. Even 15 minutes a day can lead to astonishing progress over time.

- **Weekly Review**:

   ○ Set aside time each week to reflect on your progress and adjust your plan accordingly.

- **Feedback Loops**:

   ○ Seek feedback from trusted peers or mentors to gain insights and perspective.

- **Celebrate Milestones**:

   ○ Recognize and reward yourself for the progress made, no matter how small, to maintain motivation.

- **Adjust and Evolve**:

   ○ If a certain approach isn't working, don't be afraid to tweak your strategy. Adaptability is a key component of success in personal development.

In closing, remember that the journey is as significant as the destination. As you master time management in the purview of personal development, you'll find that your confidence and self-esteem naturally soar. Let's embark on this transformative adventure with zeal, armed with the assurance that every step forward is a stepping stone to becoming the best version of yourself.

CREATING CONFIDENCE RITUALS: DAILY HABITS FOR A POWERFUL MINDSET

The Science Behind It

Confidence is not just a feeling; it's a state of being that can be developed with practice and consistency. There is a substantial body of research that supports the concept of 'neuroplasticity'—the ability of our brains to change and adapt through experience. By establishing daily habits, or 'confidence rituals,' you can effectively rewire your brain to foster a more powerful mindset. When you perform a ritual, your brain releases dopamine, a neurotransmitter associated with pleasure and motivation. This release can create positive reinforcement, making it more likely that you'll stick with the habit. Furthermore, rituals reduce anxiety by providing structure and predictability, thus creating a sense of control and competence—key ingredients for confidence.

Practical Implementation

To begin crafting your confidence rituals, consider these guidelines:

1. **Start Small**:

    ◦ Choose one or two simple activities that you can do every day without feeling overwhelmed.

    ◦ Example: Begin your morning with a five-minute meditation focusing on gratitude and self-appreciation.

2. **Personalize Your Ritual**:

    ◦ Your rituals should resonate with you and align with your personal goals.

    ◦ Example: If public speaking is a goal, practice a two-minute speech in front of a mirror each day.

3. **Incorporate Mindfulness**:

    ◦ Be present during your rituals to create a deeper connection and maximize their impact.

    ◦ Example: During a morning jog, concentrate on your breathing and the movement of your body.

4. **Visual and Affirmative Cues**:

    ◦ Use visual reminders or affirmations to stay motivated and create a vivid mental image of your confident self.

    ◦ Example: Post an inspirational quote where you'll see it every day or repeat empowering affirmations.

5. **Physical Activity**:

  ○ Exercise can increase endorphins, which boost mood and self-esteem.

  ○ Example: Incorporate a daily 10-minute workout or a brisk walk into your routine.

By introducing these activities into your daily life, you can start to establish patterns that reinforce your confidence.

Consistency and Evaluation

The key to making confidence rituals work is consistency. It takes time to form a new habit—studies suggest anywhere from 18 to 254 days, with an average of 66 days for a new behavior to become automatic. Regularity turns actions into habits, and habits into automatic behaviors that fuel your confidence without conscious effort.

To evaluate the effectiveness of your rituals, ask yourself the following questions:

• Have I felt more confident taking on new challenges?

• Are my rituals making me feel more in control and competent?

• Is my self-talk more positive?

Adjust your rituals as needed based on your responses. The beauty of these rituals is their flexibility—what matters is that they work for you.

Remember, building confidence is a journey. Be patient with yourself, and don't forget to celebrate your small victories along the way.

Engage with Your Rituals

- Tell a story about someone who overcame a confidence hurdle using these rituals.

- Create challenges for your readers to push their boundaries.

- Invite readers to share their personalized rituals and successes with the community.

By bringing these practices into your life and understanding the science behind them, you create a powerful toolkit for building a resilient and confident mindset. Your contribution to your confidence is a daily commitment, and with each ritual, you take another step towards the powerful, assured you.

LEARNING NEW SKILLS: BUILDING COMPETENCE AND ASSURANCE

In this journey of transformation, learning new skills is more than acquiring knowledge; it's about enhancing your competence and, by extension, bolstering your self-assurance. Let's dive into the fascinating process of skill acquisition and discover how it can become a cornerstone in your quest for a more confident self.

The Science Behind It

At the heart of learning new skills is the development of neural pathways in the brain. When you learn something new, your brain builds connections between neurons, and with repeated practice, these pathways become stronger, leading to increased proficiency and confidence.

Cognitive Stages of Skill Acquisition

1. **Cognitive Stage**: This involves understanding the skill and its components. Mistakes are common, but essential for learning.

2. **Associative Stage**: With practice, errors reduce, and the skill becomes more integrated. This is where improvement speeds up.

3. **Autonomous Stage**: The skill becomes second nature, allowing you to perform it with little conscious thought.

The Role of Self-Efficacy

Self-efficacy, a term coined by psychologist Albert Bandura, plays a crucial role. It refers to your belief in your ability to succeed in specific situations. As you learn and master new skills, your self-efficacy grows, leading to increased confidence in your abilities.

Practical Implementation

To effectively learn new skills, take these practical steps:

1. **Identify**: Start by pinpointing the skills that will have the most significant impact on your personal and professional life.

2. **Research**: Gather resources and tools needed for learning, such as books, online courses, or expert advice.

3. **Plan**: Create a structured learning path with short-term goals leading up to the main objective.

4. **Practice**: Engage in deliberate practice consistently, with a focus on areas that challenge you.

5. **Feedback**: Seek constructive feedback to refine your approach and improve faster.

6. **Reflect**: Take time to reflect on what you've learned and how far you've come.

Consistency and Evaluation

To solidify new skills and build assurance, follow these guidelines:

1. **Consistency**: Practice regularly. Consistent action turns effort into habit and proficiency.

2. **Tracking Progress**: Use a journal or app to track your progress. Visual growth can be a significant confidence booster.

3. **Adaptability**: Be willing to adapt your approach based on what you're learning about yourself and the skill.

4. **Evaluation**: Regularly evaluate your performance against the goals you've set, and adjust as necessary.

Real-life Example: Learning Public Speaking

Let's say you want to improve at public speaking:

• Start by understanding the basics of effective communication.

• Practice your speeches in front of a mirror or a supportive peer group.

• Incorporate feedback, and notice your growing ease in front of an audience.

• With every speech delivered, journal your experiences, noting areas of improvement and newfound confidence.

Learning new skills isn't just about the skills themselves; it's about the journey of personal growth that comes with them. As you embark on this journey, your self-esteem will rise with your competence, leading to a more confident and fulfilled you. Go forth and confidently embrace the learning process, for each new skill is a stepping stone on the path to a more assured self.

THE POWER OF BODY MOVEMENT: CONFIDENCE THROUGH PHYSICAL ACTIVITY

Confidence isn't just a state of mind—it's a physical state, too. Our bodies and minds are intrinsically linked, and movement is a powerful tool to strengthen that connection. In this chapter, we'll explore the science behind how body movement influences confidence, discover practical ways to build confidence through physical activity, and discuss strategies to maintain and evaluate these practices for long-term success.

The Science Behind It

Movement has an extraordinary impact on our brain chemistry and structure. When we exercise or simply move our bodies purposefully, several things happen:

- **Endorphin Release**: Exercise stimulates endorphin production, known as 'feel-good hormones' which promote a sense of well-being and pain relief.

- **Increased Brain Plasticity**: Regular physical activity enhances neuroplasticity, the brain's ability to form and reorganize synaptic connections.

- **Stress Reduction**: Movement helps in reducing levels of the body's stress hormones, adrenaline, and cortisol.

• **Improved Self-Perception**: When we see and feel ourselves becoming stronger and more capable, our self-perception improves.

Moreover, certain postures and movements can have an immediate effect on our confidence levels. Amy Cuddy's research on 'power posing'—adopting expansive postures to increase feelings of power and dominance—suggests that our body language can impact not only how others perceive us but also how we perceive ourselves.

Practical Implementation

Here are ways to embed physical activity into your routine to bolster confidence:

1. **Power Posing**: Start your day with a two-minute power pose. Stand tall, hands on hips, and feet apart

2. embody a superhero stance. This can prime your brain for a confident day.

3. **Exercise Regularly**: Incorporate a mix of cardiovascular exercises, strength training, and flexibility exercises into your weekly schedule.

4. **Dance**: Dance has been shown to improve coordination, body image, and social skills—all key confidence boosters.

5. **Posture Checks**: Throughout the day, perform regular posture checks—align your spine, roll your shoulders back, and keep your chin up.

6. **Yoga and Tai Chi**: Both are excellent for improving balance, focus, and a calm mind.

7. **Mindful Walking**: Use walking as a meditative practice. Focus on your stride, the movement of your arms, and the rhythm of your breath.

Consistency and Evaluation

The key to building lasting confidence through body movement is consistency and evaluation. Here's how you can ensure you stay on track:

- **Set Clear Goals**: Whether it's daily step counts or mastering a new dance routine, having clear, achievable goals will keep you motivated.

- **Monitor Progress**: Keep a record of your physical activity and note down how you feel before and after. Reflect on changes in your confidence levels over time.

- **Build Habit Triggers**: Associate physical activity with specific cues (e.g., after brushing your teeth, go for a walk) to develop habits.

- **Seek Feedback**: Share your goals with friends or coaches and regularly ask for feedback.

Remember, building confidence through movement doesn't happen overnight. It's about small daily actions that add up to significant changes in how you feel about yourself. Prioritize movement, and watch as your confidence grows, one step, one pose, one dance at a time.

MINDFULNESS AND MEDITATION: ANCHORING SELF-ASSURANCE IN THE PRESENT MOMENT

In our fast-paced world, confidence can sometimes feel like a scarce commodity. The consistent pressures and expectations to perform can erode our self-assurance. Yet, a potent antidote lies within our reach. This chapter delves into how mindfulness and meditation can be the cornerstone of a confident and grounded existence.

The Science Behind It

Mindfulness and meditation aren't just spiritual concepts; they are backed by science. Research has unveiled a myriad of ways in which these practices can bolster our mental fortitude.

- **Neuroplasticity:** Regular mindfulness practice can actually change brain structures responsible for attention, emotion regulation, and self-awareness.

- **Stress Reduction:** Meditation triggers the body's relaxation response, offsetting the stress hormone cortisol and promoting a state of calmness.

- **Enhanced Focus:** Mindfulness aids in reducing mind-wandering and improving concentration, which are crucial in building and maintaining confidence in one's abilities.

- **Emotional Resilience:** By observing our emotions without judgment, mindfulness allows us to develop a buffer against negativity and to bounce back more effectively from setbacks.

Practical Implementation

Transforming abstract concepts into daily habits is where the true power lies. Here's how to weave mindfulness and meditation into the fabric of your life:

- **Start Small:** Begin with just five minutes of meditation each day. All you need is a quiet space where you won't be disturbed.

- **Use Guides:** Leverage guided meditations available online or via apps to help you stay focused and learn various techniques.

- **Integrate Mindfulness:** Practice being fully present during everyday tasks – such as while eating or walking. Note the sights, sounds, and sensations you experience.

- **Mindful Breathing:** Whenever you feel overwhelmed, take a moment to focus solely on your breathing. This anchors you in the present and can be a quick confidence booster.

Mindfulness Techniques

- **Body Scan Meditation:** Mentally traverse through your body, noting any sensations or discomforts. This increases body awareness and reduces anxiety.

- **Loving-Kindness Meditation:** Send positive wishes to yourself and others. This practice can enhance feelings of self-worth and empathy.

- **Mindful Observation:** Pick an object and observe it intently, noting every detail. This improves focus and presence.

Consistency and Evaluation

Consistent practice compounds benefits. Daily meditation leads to improved self-assurance that can weather the highs and lows of life. Evaluating your progress can help reinforce the habit. Ask yourself:

- Have my stress levels decreased?

- Is my focus sharper in high-pressure situations?

- Do I rebound from disappointments more resiliently?

Tracking Progress

1. **Journaling:** Making a note of your experiences can provide insight into your progress and can serve as motivation.

2. **Set Milestones:** Mark specific intervals, like one week, one month, and so forth to evaluate changes in your confidence levels.

3. **Feedback Loops:** Don't shy away from asking close friends or colleagues if they've noticed a change. External perspectives can be illuminating.

Incorporating mindfulness and meditation into your life isn't just about silencing the mind – it's about empowering the self. As you anchor yourself in the present moment, each breath becomes a reaffirmation of your capabilities and worth. With time, the roots of self-assurance deepen, and the fruits of confidence flourish.

THE ROLE OF NUTRITION: FUELING YOUR BODY AND MIND FOR CONFIDENCE

The Science Behind It

Nutrition is the cornerstone of our health, impacting our bodies and minds in substantial ways. A well-balanced diet provides the energy we need to tackle daily tasks but also plays a pivotal role in maintaining a confident mindset. Let's delve into the scientific link between what we consume and our self-assurance.

- **Energy Levels**: Whole foods rich in complex carbohydrates, lean proteins, and healthy fats provide sustained energy, which is crucial for confidence. If we're energized, we're more likely to engage actively in our pursuits.

- **Mood Regulation**: Certain nutrients, like omega-3 fatty acids and vitamin D, have been linked to mood stabilization. A stable mood fosters a positive outlook, making challenges seem more manageable.

- **Cognitive Function**: Foods high in antioxidants and flavonoids can enhance memory and cognitive speed, helping us feel sharp and on top of our game.

- **Stress Reduction**: B vitamins, magnesium, and the amino acid tryptophan assist in reducing stress levels, a common confidence killer.

Through these mechanisms, a nutritious diet doesn't just fuel our bodies; it primes our mental engine, too, allowing us to navigate life with a firmer belief in our capabilities.

Practical Implementation

Here are ways to align your eating habits with the path to heightened confidence:

1. **Start with Breakfast**: A protein-rich breakfast can set the tone for the day, enhancing alertness and curbing cravings.

2. **Hydration**: Keeping well-hydrated ensures that energy levels don't dip. Aim for clear or pale yellow urine as a sign you're drinking enough.

3. **Mindful Eating**: Pay attention to your body's hunger and fullness cues. Eating mindfully can prevent overeating, which often leads to discomfort and decreases confidence.

4. **Incremental Changes**: Make small dietary adjustments rather than drastic ones. Gradual improvements are sustainable and less overwhelming.

5. **Plan Your Meals**: By planning meals, you can ensure a balanced intake of nutrients, fostering both physical and mental health.

By integrating these habits, you can construct a dietary pattern that serves as the foundation for continued personal growth and self-esteem.

Consistency and Evaluation

Building a routine is essential. Here's how to stay consistent and measure your progress.

- **Food Journaling**: Keep a record of what you eat and how you feel. Over time, patterns will emerge, showing the link between certain foods and your self-confidence levels.

- **Regular Check-ins**: Set weekly or monthly check-ins to review your diet and emotional well-being. Adjust as necessary.

- **Smart Goal Setting**: Make SMART (Specific, Measurable, Achievable, Relevant, Time-Bound) goals to continuously aim for a diet that enhances confidence.

Embrace the journey of nutritional improvement knowing it has profound benefits, not just for your body, but for your self-esteem and confidence as well.

DRESSING FOR SUCCESS: THE IMPACT OF APPEARANCE ON CONFIDENCE

The Science Behind It

Psychological Influence of Clothing

Dressing for success isn't just about looking good for others—it's about feeling good about yourself. The phenomenon known as 'enclothed cognition' suggests that the clothes we wear have a direct impact on our psychological processes. This not only affects the way others perceive us but also how we perceive ourselves.

- **Enclothed Cognition:** Studies show that when individuals don a white lab coat associated with scientists, they tend to perform better on attention-related tasks, linking their attire to an increased level of attentiveness.

- **Self-Perception Theory:** The clothes we wear can influence our thoughts, feelings, and behavior, much like how actors may embody characteristics of a role through costume.

- **Symbolic Meaning:** The symbolism of our clothing, be it power, professionalism, or playfulness, can shift our attitude and performance accordingly.

Confidence-Boosting Effects of Dress

Attire can be a powerful tool in bolstering self-confidence:

• **Visual Competence:** Well-fitted and appropriate clothing can enhance the perception of competence and expertise.

• **Self-Alignment:** When outward appearance aligns with personal and professional identity, it reinforces a sense of self-assuredness.

• **Mood Regulation:** Wearing clothes that you associate with positive experiences can improve mood and confidence.

Practical Implementation

To harness the power of dressing well, follow these actionable advice:

1. Understand Your Environment:

   ○ Dress to match the expectations and norms of your workplace or social setting to harness contextual confidence.

2. Know Your Colors:

   ○ Identify colors that complement your skin tone, hair, and eyes, enhancing your natural features and boosting confidence.

3. Prioritize Fit and Comfort:

   ○ Ensure your clothing fits well and is comfortable; this indicates you value yourself, promoting both comfort and competence.

4. Personal Style as Expression:

   ○ Develop a personal style that reflects your personality; this authenticity can be a significant confidence booster.

5. Quality Over Quantity:

   ◦ Investing in a few high-quality pieces rather than many low-quality items can help maintain a consistent, confident image.

Consistency and Evaluation

Consistency in your dressing habits helps solidify the positive effects on confidence. Here's how you can maintain it:

- **Seasonal Audit:** Every season, assess your wardrobe to ensure it still meets your personal and professional needs.

- **Milestone Reflection:** After key events or periods, reflect on how your attire might have influenced your confidence levels.

Finally, evaluation of your dressing choices and their outcomes is crucial:

1. Seek Feedback:

   ◦ Ask peers for their honest opinions on how your attire impacts your presence and confidence.

2. Self-Assessment:

   ◦ Regularly note down how different outfits make you feel and perform, modifying your wardrobe choices as needed.

3. Adjust and Adapt:

   ◦ Be open to altering your clothing choices as your personal and professional goals evolve.

Remember, dressing for success is a continuous journey of aligning your external appearance with your confidence and competence. Using these strategies will ensure that every day you are well-dressed, is a day you are well-addressed.

THE CONFIDENCE-SUCCESS CYCLE: BUILDING MOMENTUM

The Science Behind It

Confidence and success are interlinked in a dynamic cycle that often determines personal growth and achievement. Scientific research indicates that individuals who exude confidence are likely to take more risks and seize opportunities—all pivotal actions for achieving success. Let's delve into what fuels this cycle:

- **Self-Efficacy Theory**: Developed by psychologist Albert Bandura, this theory suggests that believing in your own ability to succeed impacts your willingness to face challenges.

- **Positive Feedback Loops**: As you achieve small successes, you receive internal and external validation, which boosts your confidence and incentivizes further efforts.

- **Neuroplasticity**: Your brain adapts to your experiences; success and confidence can help rewire your brain to expect positive outcomes, creating a 'success mindset.'

Understanding this cycle illuminates why building momentum through confidence can lead to continued success.

Practical Implementation

But how are these scientific insights applied to everyday life? Here are steps to start the cycle:

1. **Set Achievable Goals**: Aim for low-hanging fruit at first—achieving these will give you an initial confidence boost.

2. **Prepare and Plan**: Equipping yourself with knowledge and resources increases the probability of success.

3. **Visualize Success**: The act of visualization can build neural pathways associated with actual achievement.

4. **Positive Affirmations**: These help to reinforce self-belief and confidence.

5. **Celebrate Successes**: No matter how small, celebrating achievements reinforces the cycle of confidence and success.

Remember, every big triumph comprises numerous small victories.

Consistency and Evaluation

Maintaining momentum is critical in reinforcing the confidence-success cycle. Here are strategies to ensure consistency:

- **Habit Formation**: Integrate activities that build confidence into your daily routine, making them automatic responses rather than conscious efforts.

- **Reflective Practice**: Regularly assess what's working and what isn't, and adjust your approach accordingly.

- **Seek Feedback**: Constructive criticism can reveal blind spots and offer opportunities for improvement.

Real-World Illustrations

Consider J.K. Rowling, who, despite countless rejections, confidently pursued publishing until *Harry Potter * became a global success. Or, think of small business owners who leverage initial successes into sustained growth. These narratives exemplify the cycle in action.

A Balanced View

While confidence does contribute to success, it's essential to remain grounded. Overconfidence can lead to taking unnecessary risks, so balance optimism with realism. Evaluating your capabilities accurately and adjusting your actions is just as important as fostering a confidence mindset.
By nurturing this confidence-success cycle with intentionality, persistence, and a touch of humility, anyone can build the momentum necessary to achieve their personal and professional goals.

CELEBRATING YOUR ACHIEVEMENTS: SELF-RECOGNITION AND REWARD

In our journey toward personal growth and bolstering self-confidence, acknowledging our own successes is a pivotal step. This chapter takes you through the science-backed reasons why celebrating your achievements can build self-esteem and provides practical strategies for incorporating self-recognition into your life.

The Science Behind It

It's not just about feeling good; there's substantial evidence indicating that self-recognition has tangible benefits.

- **Dopamine Release**: Accomplishing goals triggers the release of dopamine, the 'feel-good' neurotransmitter. This chemical reaction creates a sense of pleasure and reinforces behaviors that lead to success.

- **Positive Reinforcement**: Psychologically, when we celebrate, we're engaging in positive reinforcement. This conditions us to repeat the actions and behaviors that lead to the rewarding experience.

- **Self-Efficacy**: Bandura's theory of self-efficacy suggests that individuals who believe in their ability to accomplish tasks are more likely to take on challenges and persist in the face of setbacks. Celebrating achievements boosts this belief.

• **Goal-Setting Theory**: According to Locke and Latham's goal-setting theory, clear goals and appropriate feedback contribute to higher and better task performance. Celebrating wins can serve as valuable feedback.

Practical Implementation

Implementing self-recognition in our daily routines can be simple yet powerful. Here are some ways to do so:

1. **Create a Success Journal**: Keep a record of your triumphs, whether it's a secured business deal or a newfound personal habit.

    ○ Write accomplishments in a bullet-point format for clarity.

    ○ Include how you felt and the steps you took to achieve each goal!

2. **Set Specific Milestones**: Divide large goals into smaller, manageable milestones.

    ○ Celebrate when each mini-goal is reached, no matter how small.

3. **Reward Yourself**: Pair your successes with meaningful rewards.

    ○ Whether it's a nice meal, a new book, or even a day off, choose rewards that resonate with you.

4. **Share Your Triumphs**: Sometimes, celebrating with others can magnify the joy.

    ○ Organize small get-togethers or share your achievements with a close friend.

5. **Visual Representation**: Create a visual board or chart to track progress.

  ○ Seeing the progression can invigorate your drive and confidence.

Consistency and Evaluation

Like any other personal growth practice, consistency in self-recognition is key.

• **Regular Check-Ins**: Set aside time weekly or monthly for reflection and celebration of accomplishments.

• **Progressive Goals**: As you grow, your capacity for achievement does too. Ensure your milestones evolve with your skills.

• **Evaluation**: Look back on your journal and visual trackers.

  ○ Evaluate what worked, what didn't, and strategize for future endeavors.

Let's remember, celebrating achievements is more than self-indulgence; it's an essential strategy for long-term personal growth and robust self-esteem. Take pride in your journey and every small victory along the way. As you embark on the 42-day path to a more confident you, let self-recognition be the wind beneath your wings propelling you upward and onward.

BEING A ROLE MODEL: INSPIRING CONFIDENCE IN OTHERS

The Science Behind It

As a society, we often look up to those we consider role models to guide our behaviors and attitudes. But what is the basis for the influence these individuals have? Psychological studies suggest a few core principles:

- **Social Learning Theory**: As Bandura's work illustrates, we learn by observing and emulating the behaviors of others. When individuals see a role model demonstrating confidence, they are likely to imitate this trait.

- **Mirror Neurons**: These neurons fire both when we act and when we observe the same action performed by others, providing a neuroscientific basis for empathy and learning from role models.

- **Self-Efficacy**: According to Bandura, witnessing others successfully achieving goals can bolster an individual's belief in their own abilities.

Practical Implementation

To become an effective role model and inspire confidence in others, consider the following strategies:

1. **Emphasize Positive Attributes**: Highlight your strengths and accomplishments without arrogance. This can create an aspirational image for others to follow.

2. **Display Resilience**: Show that you can bounce back from setbacks, reinforcing the idea that confidence is not about never failing, but about persisting through challenges.

3. **Communicate Effectively**: Use positive language and active listening skills to engage with others in a manner that fosters mutual respect.

4. **Set Clear Goals**: Demonstrate the importance of goal-setting by sharing your own objectives and the steps you are taking to achieve them.

5. **Encourage Others**: Provide support and constructive feedback that can help others develop their skills and confidence.

Consistency and Evaluation

Developing into a role model who can inspire confidence in others requires consistent behavior. To assess your impact:

- Reflect on feedback from those around you about whether your actions are indeed fostering confidence.

- Evaluate whether your interactions are consistent with the values you wish to transmit.

- Regularly revisit your goals and strategies to ensure they align with being an inspiring role model.

By fostering confidence in others, role models become agents of positive change, often creating a ripple effect that can impact entire communities. With careful attention and dedication to the principles outlined in this chapter, anyone can aspire to be such an influential figure.

Remember, the essence of being a role model lies not in perfection, but in the authentic demonstration of striving for personal growth and excellence. Keep inspiring!

THE LIFELONG JOURNEY: MAINTAINING AND GROWING YOUR CONFIDENCE

The Science Behind It

Confidence isn't just a feeling; it's a psychological state backed by a chorus of neural symphonies and hormonal responses within our bodies. When you experience a boost in confidence, your body releases a dash of neurotransmitters like dopamine, which not only makes you feel good but also primes your brain for peak performance. Studies have shown that confidence can increase your ability to focus, make decisions, and manage stress. However, this delightful cocktail of neurochemicals isn't life's free pour. It takes practice to cultivate, much like a skill. Many psychologists endorse the theory that confidence is indeed a learned behavior, which can be strengthened over time through repeated exposure to challenging situations, constructive feedback, and positive reinforcement.

Practical Implementation

Foster a Growth Mindset

- **Embrace challenges**: Seeing challenges as opportunities to grow can increase resilience. Instead of backing away from difficult tasks, lean into them with a sense of curiosity.

• **Learn from feedback**: Take criticism constructively, not personally. Every piece of feedback is a golden nugget towards your self-improvement.

• **Celebrate the small wins**: Confidence builds up gradually. Recognize and rejoice in the incremental progress you make every day.

Surround Yourself With Confidence Catalysts

• **Seek inspiring company**: Spend time with people who inspire you and exude the confidence you aspire to have.

• **Find a mentor**: A seasoned guide can bolster your belief in yourself by sharing their wisdom and experience.

• **Engage in positive self-talk**: Your internal dialogue has immense power. Replace negative thoughts with affirmations that reinforce your self-worth.

Keep Learning and Improving

• **Acquire new skills**: Continuous learning keeps your mind sharp and your skill set relevant, both of which can bolster your confidence.

• **Stay well-informed**: Having a firm grasp of what's happening in your field or the world at large can make you feel more poised and in control.

Consistency and Evaluation

Maintaining and growing confidence is a perpetual process. It requires you to be consistent in your endeavors and periodically evaluate your progress.

- **Set measurable goals**: Define what confidence looks like for you, and break it down into achievable milestones.

- **Reflect on progress**: Regularly look back at where you started and how far you've come to appreciate your journey.

- **Adjust your tactics**: If certain strategies aren't serving you well, be prepared to adapt your approach.

In the realm of confidence, static is synonymous with stagnation. You must constantly challenge yourself to step out of your comfort zone, make room for growth, and evaluate the efficacy of your strategies.

Maintaining and growing confidence is not a sprint; it's a lifelong marathon. Shifts in self-esteem are inevitable, but with the right mindset, strategies, and consistent effort, you can cultivate a wellspring of confidence that endures the highs and lows of life's journey.

GIVING BACK: THE ROLE OF ALTRUISM IN SELF-ESTEEM

The Science Behind It

Altruism, the selfless concern for the well-being of others, has been scrutinized through the lens of psychology and neuroscience to reveal its surprising impact on self-esteem. Let's delve into the mechanics of how giving back can boost our internal sense of self-worth.

- **Positive Feedback Loop**: Engaging in altruistic behaviors triggers a release of endorphins, known as the "helper's high," bringing about a feel-good state that reinforces further acts of kindness.

- **Social Connectivity**: Altruism often increases our sense of social connection, an essential component of self-esteem, as we are naturally social creatures who thrive on meaningful interpersonal relationships.

- **Moral Elevation**: Witnessing acts of kindness can lead to moral elevation, fostering inspiration to do good ourselves, which in turn enhances self-regard.

In essence, when we shift our focus away from ourselves and towards the needs of others, our own self-view improves, often unexpectedly so.

Practical Implementation

To incorporate the benefits of altruism into your life, consider the following actionable steps:

1. **Volunteering**: Dedicate a portion of your time to a local community service. This can range from helping at a soup kitchen to tutoring children in need.

2. **Acts of Kindness**: Make it a daily habit to perform small, random acts of kindness. These could be as simple as holding the door open for someone or paying a compliment.

3. **Charitable Giving**: Donate to causes that resonate with you. Remember, generosity is not measured by the amount but by the spirit of the contribution.

By doing these activities, not only are you contributing tangibly to the well-being of others, but you are also nurturing your own self-esteem through consistent, purposeful action.

Consistency and Evaluation

Maintaining regular altruistic actions and reflecting on their impact is important for sustained self-esteem growth.

- Keep a **Kindness Journal** to record your acts of giving back and note any shifts in your feelings of self-worth.

- Set **Altruistic Goals** for yourself each week or month to build a habit of giving.

- **Reflect on Your Experiences** with peers or mentors to gain insights and stay motivated.

Engagement Strategies

• Share your journey of altruism with friends or through social media to inspire others and create an accountability loop for yourself.

• Partner with charities or organizations and become a long-term advocate for a cause, helping you integrate altruism deeper into your life's purpose.

By consistently applying these practices and evaluating their outcomes, you integrate the principles of altruism into your life and create a stable foundation for self-esteem that can weather life's challenges.
Altruism isn't just about giving back; it's about intertwining our lives with the greater fabric of humanity. Through it, we realize that we gain not just the gratitude of others but an enduring respect for ourselves that carries through every facet of our personal and professional lives.

YOUR CONFIDENT FUTURE: ENVISIONING AND EMBRACING YOUR BEST SELF

The Science Behind It

It's no secret that confidence plays a pivotal role in our ability to navigate life's challenges and opportunities. However, it isn't just a feel-good state of mind; it's a psychological construct with well-documented neuroscientific and behavioral research to back it up.

- **Neuroplasticity**: Our brains are inherently plastic, meaning they can rewire themselves through thoughts and experiences. Engaging in positive visualization and affirmation exercises can literally reshape the pathways in our brains, leading to increased confidence.

- **Self-perception Theory**: This theory posits that we often determine our inner feelings from our external behaviors. If we act confidently, we begin to view ourselves as confident individuals.

- **Self-efficacy**: Coined by psychologist Albert Bandura, self-efficacy refers to our belief in our ability to succeed. Strengthening our self-efficacy through mastery experiences, social modeling, and managing physiological responses is key to cultivating confidence.

Practical Implementation

To transform your scientific understanding into a real-world confidence boost, let's explore some actionable strategies:

1. **Vision Board Creation**: Make a collage representative of your goals and dreams. This visual reminder can inspire and motivate you to act with confidence.

2. **Affirmation Practice**: Develop a set of personal affirmations that you resonate with, and recite them daily. This repetition reinforces positive self-perception.

3. **Role Modeling**: Identify individuals who embody the confidence you aspire to achieve. Observe how they navigate the world and what you can learn from them.

4. **Skill Development**: Take on new challenges to master new skills, enhancing your sense of self-efficacy with each success.

5. **Mindfulness Exercises**: Engage in mindfulness to manage stress and anxiety, thereby reducing the physiological symptoms that can undermine confidence.

Consistency and Evaluation

To truly embody a confident persona, consistency in these practices is critical. Likewise, periodic self-evaluation ensures that you're not only staying on track but also recognizing and celebrating your growth.

- **Daily Rituals**: Integrate your confidence-building activities into your everyday routine, making them as habitual as brushing your teeth.

- **Growth Journal**: Keep a journal to reflect on your progress and setbacks. This record will help you adjust your strategies and recognize patterns in your behavior.

- **Feedback Loops**: Seek constructive feedback from trusted peers to gain external perspective on your confidence journey.

In conclusion, a confident future is not just a dream—it's a destination that you can reach through understanding the science, implementing practical strategies, and committing to consistent self-evaluation. Armed with this knowledge, you are well on your way to becoming your best, most confident self.